GODS OF THE ANDES

GODS OF THE ANDES

An Early Jesuit Account of Inca Religion and Andean Christianity

Sabine Hyland

The Pennsylvania State University Press
University Park, Pennsylvania

The map of western South America facing p. 1 is
reprinted from Sabine Hyland, *The Jesuit and the
Incas: The Extraordinary Life of Padre Blas Valera, S.J.*,
by permission of the University of Michigan Press.
Copyright © by the University of Michigan 2003.

Library of Congress Cataloging-in-Publication Data
Valera, Blas, 1551–1597.
[De las costumbres antiguas de los naturales del Pirʻ.
English]
Gods of the Andes : an early Jesuit account of Inca
religion and Andean Christianity / [edited by]
Sabine Hyland.
    p.   cm.—(Latin American originals)
Includes bibliographical references and index.
Summary: "An English translation of a sixteenth-
century Spanish manuscript, by an Inca Jesuit, about
Inca religion and the spread of Christianity in colonial
Peru. Includes an introductory essay"—Provided by
publisher.
ISBN 978-0-271-04880-2 (pbk. : alk. paper)
1. Incas—Religion—Early works to 1800.
2. Incas—Rites and ceremonies—Early works to 1800.
3. Peru—Church history—16th century—Early
works to 1800.
I. Hyland, Sabine, 1964– .
II. Title.

F3429.3.R3V3513 2011
299.8—dc22
2011002908

It is the policy of The Pennsylvania State University
Press to use acid-free paper. Publications on uncoated
stock satisfy the minimum requirements of American
National Standard for Information Sciences—
Permanence of Paper for Printed Library Material,
ANSI Z39.48–1992.

CONTENTS

Preface   ix

Acknowledgments   xi

Map   xii

1   Native Gods and Missionaries   1

2   Blas Valera: His Life and "Crimes"   17

3   Sources   35

Notes Concerning This Translation   47

Blas Valera, *An Account of the Ancient Customs of the Natives of Peru*   49

Appendix   105

Glossary of Quechua Terms   111

Works Cited   114

Index   121

Latin American Originals (LAO) is a series of primary source texts on colonial Latin America. LAO volumes are accessible, affordable editions of texts translated into English—most of them for the very first time, as is the case with LAO 6. The first half-dozen books in the series illuminate aspects of the Spanish conquests during the century from the 1520s to the 1610s.

Taken in the chronological order of their primary texts, LAO 2, *Invading Guatemala*, shows how reading multiple accounts of conquest wars (in this case, Spanish, Nahua, and Maya versions of the Guatemalan conflict of the 1520s) can explode established narratives and suggest a conquest story that is more complicated, disturbing, and revealing. LAO 1, *Invading Colombia*, challenges us to view the difficult Spanish invasion of Colombia in the 1530s as more representative of conquest campaigns than the better-known assaults on the Mexica and Inca empires. LAO 3, *The Conquest on Trial*, features a fictional embassy of indigenous Americans filing a complaint over the conquest in a court in Spain—the Court of Death. That text, the first theatrical examination of the conquest published in Spain, effectively condenses contemporary debates on colonization into one dramatic package. LAO 4, *Defending the Conquest*, is a spirited, ill-humored, and polemic apologia for the Spanish Conquest written by a lesser-known veteran conquistador and submitted for publication—without success—in 1613. LAO 5, *Forgotten Franciscans*, offers a trio of controversial opinions on conversion processes in Mexico, written between 1543 and 1614.

LAO 6, like LAO 5, casts a surprising light on the spiritual conquest, showing how within the church in Spanish America there were wildly divergent views both on native religions and on how to replace them with Christianity. *Gods of the Andes* presents the first English edition of a 1594 manuscript describing Inca religion and the campaign to convert native Andeans. Discovered in private hands in Spain in the nineteenth century, the manuscript is attributed by scholars to Blas Valera, a Jesuit missionary who died of injuries acquired when the English sacked Cádiz in 1596. Valera is surprisingly sympathetic to pre-Conquest beliefs and practices, viewing them as preparing Andeans for the arrival of the faith he helped bring from Spain.

The source texts to LAO volumes are either archival documents—written in Spanish, Portuguese, or indigenous languages such as Nahuatl, Zapotec, and Maya—or rare books published in the colonial period in their original language (Spanish, Portuguese, Italian, Latin). The contributing authors are historians, anthropologists, art historians, and scholars of literature; they have developed a specialized knowledge that allows them to locate, translate, and present these texts in a way that contributes to scholars' understanding of the period, while also making them readable for students and nonspecialists.

Sabine Hyland is an ethnohistorian with just this kind of specialized knowledge. She has built upon an Ivy League education, a lifelong fascination with the Andean past, and an acute understanding of Jesuit and Inca history to become one of the world's leading scholars—perhaps *the* leader—on Jesuit views of the Incas. As such, she is ideally positioned to package for us Valera's intriguing take on the religious experience of the Andes in the fifteenth and sixteenth centuries.

—Matthew Restall

ACKNOWLEDGMENTS

Many people generously helped to bring this book to completion. I am especially grateful to Matthew Restall and Michael Francis, who asked me to prepare this work and who provided essential comments and support. Frank Salomon's incisive comments improved the work considerably, and I am deeply grateful to him. An anonymous reader provided extremely useful suggestions and corrections. Dave Peterson, who read an early version of the translation, offered very useful comments on the text. My daughter, Margaret, gave important feedback concerning style and clarity. My husband, Bill, has been wonderfully helpful and supportive at every stage of the manuscript, from the beginning of the project to its end. I am particularly grateful to him for supplying the translations from Latin in the original text. This book could not have been done without his support.

I owe special thanks to the family of the renowned illustrator Henry C. Pitz for allowing me to use Pitz's illustration for the cover.

Thanks to Connie Meulemans for her assiduousness in getting books for me; thanks also to the production staff at Penn State Press for their fine work, and especially to the copy editor, John Morris. Three summer research grants from the St. Norbert College Office of Faculty Development enabled this project to be completed.

Finally, I would like to thank the many people who have written me in support of my writings on Valera.

EQUATOR

Quito

Puerto Viejo

▲ Chimborazo
Riobamba

Tumebamba

Tumbez

Río Marañón

Chachapoyas

Cajamarca
Huamachuco

Trujillo
Huaylas

Río Ucayali

Huánuco

Cajatambo

Chillón
Canta   Xuaxa
Lima   Huarochirí   Río Apurímac
Pachacámac   Huamanga

Chincha

Andahuaylas   Cuzco   Urcos
Ica

Nazca

EL COLLAO
LAKE TITICACA
Chucuito

Arequipa   Copacabana   La Paz (Chuquiabo)

Sicasica   Cochabamba

La Plata
(Chuquisaca)

CHARCAS
Potosí

PACIFIC OCEAN

MAP
LOCATION

1

Native Gods and Missionaries

Sometime during the early 1600s, in an adobe house built in the rugged Andean highlands east of Lima, a high-born native man named Cristóbal Choque Casa woke up from a dream. As he recounted later, while he was asleep he had engaged in a battle with the ancient god Llocllay Huancupa, the major deity of the Huarochiri region before the arrival of Jesuit missionaries in 1570. At Llocllay's temple, atop a stepped pyramid, local peoples had given offerings of llamas, guinea pigs, clothing, and beer to their god, who in turn provided them with protection and health. Since the coming of Christianity, however, his shrine had been abandoned and had fallen into ruins, although many local villagers secretly maintained their loyalty to their ancient protector. On his deathbed, Don Cristóbal's father himself had returned to the worship of Llocllay Huancupa after spending many years upholding the Jesuits' gospel of Christ.

In Don Cristóbal's dream he had been irresistibly drawn to Llocllay Huancupa's temple. Inside an old woman reprimanded him for abandoning the god, while a priest, Astu Huaman, presented food, beer, and coca leaf to the object, perhaps a pre-Columbian artifact, representing the deity. As Don Cristóbal watched, a strange mural unfolded around the walls of the shrine, revealing alternating figures of tiny black demons and llama heads. Filled with terror at the sight of the encircling devils, Don Cristóbal challenged Llocllay to justify himself: "Listen, Llocllay Huancupa . . . why have you summoned me now? For my part I say, 'Is not Jesus Christ the son of God? Shall I not revere this one, the true God? Shall I not revere his word forever?'" When Llocllay remained mute, unable to respond to Don Cristóbal's queries, the latter shouted, "Look! Are you not a demon? Could you defeat my Lord Jesus Christ, in whom I believe? Look! This house of yours! Yes, you dwell surrounded by demons—should I believe in you?" At this, an object was thrown at Don Cristóbal, and he fled until at last he awoke. The Quechua text recounting this narrative tells us that Don Cristóbal fought with the ancient gods in his dreams many times after this (Salomon and Urioste 1991, 101–10).

Don Cristóbal's dream exemplifies the difficulties and contradictions experienced by Andean peoples as they adapted to the Christian beliefs imposed by the conquering Spaniards. Throughout the sixteenth century, the Christianization of native peoples remained a key component of Spanish rule in Peru, and missionaries were dispatched to evangelize the indigenous population. Don Cristóbal, a staunch supporter of Christianity who reprimanded his fellow villagers for their allegiance to the old gods (Salomon and Urioste 1991, 105–6), clearly believed that the ancient deities still existed and had the power to invade his dreams. What nightly torment he must have endured as he fought, terrified, with Llocllay Huancupa and the other gods evening after evening.

Some thirty years earlier, on the first Christian mission to Huarochiri, a young Jesuit named Blas Valera struggled with similar issues of how to understand the replacement of Andean religion by Christianity. The son of an Indian woman and a Spanish conquistador, Valera evinced a keen sense of loyalty to the customs and beliefs of his Andean mother. We know that while he was in Huarochiri he held discussions with Sebastián Nina Villca, a senior member of Don Cristóbal's community, over whether the Andean gods were demonic. Valera would devote many years to studying the nature of Andean religion with native leaders throughout the highlands as well as in Cuzco, the Inca capital. One of the fruits of his lifetime of labor is the text translated here: *An Account of the Ancient Customs of the Natives of Peru*.

Based on years of research by an educated writer with native fluency in Andean language and culture, the *Account* provides a rich source of information about ancient Peru not readily available elsewhere. For example, the following description of the feast held by consecrated virgins (*acllas*) after the harvest is unique:

> The virgin *acllas* came out dressed in white and red, accompanied by many lords. Beginning with the king and the queen and the crown prince, they gave abundant food to everyone. . . .
>
> Later the virgins took out all of the fine cloth that they had worked on all of that year, and offered the best and the most

unusual, of various colors and stitches, to the king and the
queen and the crown prince and the princes and princesses, if
there were any. Later they gave to each one of the lords and
principal men and to their wives and children their precious
garments, various headgear and shoes for men and women,
sashes, wreathes, jewels, brooches, handbags, and many other
things. The clothing was all from vicuña wool, which equals
silk. . . . With this act, the *acllas* gained more, because the lords
and the people gave them great presents of livestock, land, gold,
silver, wool, harvests, etc.

This colorful depiction of an important Inca ritual, with its character-
istically Andean emphasis on reciprocity, is not found anywhere else
in colonial Andean literature; it demonstrates the valuable window
into Andean customs provided by the text.

Nonetheless, despite its ethnographic importance, the *Account* is
notable for the degree to which it presents the Andean past through
the prism of Roman Catholicism. Whereas Don Cristóbal's dreams
portrayed the ancient gods as demons, Valera takes the opposite
approach. For him, Andean religion was a precursor to Christianity,
and therefore mirrored Christian beliefs and practices in many ways.
As a way of honoring the Andean faith, Valera depicts Inca religion
as a suitable *preparatio evangelica* for the spread of the Christian
gospel in Peru. This attitude occasionally leads Valera to distort
aspects of Inca practice to make them conform to Christian ideals. For
example, he describes the chief priest of the empire, the *Vilahoma*,
as living like "a monk" by spending most of his time in solitude,
far from populated areas, the better to contemplate the gods. In fact,
the *Vilahoma* lived permanently at the Coricancha (Golden Enclo-
sure) Temple, in the heart of Cuzco, where he exercised a central role
in Inca politics (see, for example, Betanzos 1996, 45–49; 280–81; Cieza
de León 1985, 99). Likewise, Valera denies that the Incas practiced
human sacrifice, although there exists archaeological and written evidence that human sacrifice in fact occurred in the Inca Empire, albeit
on a relatively small scale.[1] Such distortions in the presentation of

1. Joahan Reinhard has discovered the mummified remains of several human
sacrificial victims on high peaks in the Southern Andes (Reinhard 2006). The Incas'
primary ritual of human sacrifice was the *Qhapaq ucha* ceremony, performed at major
events such as the ascension of the emperor. According to Spanish chroniclers, during

Inca religion had a clearly polemical purpose. Valera's intention was to prove to his readers that Andean religion was imbued with virtue and that, moreover, Andean customs should be integrated into Peruvian Christianity. Part ethnography, part apologetics for the inherent worth of the Andean past, *An Account of the Ancient Customs of the Natives of Peru* provides irreplaceable insights into religion in the Andes both before and after the Spanish conquest of Peru.

An Account of the Ancient Customs of the Natives of Peru

The anonymous manuscript entitled *De las costumbres antiguas de los naturales del Piru* (*An Account of the Ancient Customs of the Natives of Peru*) came to the attention of the scholarly world in 1836, when it was discovered in the private collection of Böhl de Faber in Cadiz. Today this eighty-three-page manuscript, the sole colonial version of the text, is housed in the Biblioteca Nacional in Madrid (Ms. # 3177). Examination of the original manuscript reveals it to be a separate work in its own right and not merely a portion of a longer text. Extensive marginalia in the earlier pages include citations to other authorities, additional arguments, and supplemental information, such as the appropriate Quechua terms for items in the main text. While the body of the text is written in one hand, the marginal notations and corrections are in at least one and possibly two other hands.[2] The date of the manuscript can be determined by a statement in the text that the Jesuits had sent two missions to Chachapoyas and that the second one was twelve years earlier. The Jesuits' first mission to Chachapoyas was in 1576, and the second one was in 1582 (see

---

this ceremony offerings were made at all the shrines and holy places (*huaca*) in the empire, including at each of the over three hundred shrines of the sacred network of *ceque* shrines around Cuzco. Children were sacrificed only at the most important of the shrines, such as at the high peaks. The current state of archaeological research suggests that human sacrifice did not occur at most shrines. In Brian Bauer's archeological survey of the *ceque* shrines of Cuzco, for example, he found evidence of human burial at only three shrines; nothing approaching the thousands of victims described by the Spanish chroniclers has been reported in the archaeological record (Bauer 1998; D'Altroy 2002, 169–73). The *Account* may well be correct in stating that the Incas usually sacrificed animals in the name of humans.

2. Personal communication from Professor James J. John, professor emeritus of paleography, Cornell University, October 1998.

Monumenta peruana 1966–86, 4:615n29), giving 1594 as the earliest possible date for the composition of the *Account*.

Although the text is anonymous, scholars unanimously agree that it was written by a Jesuit. Not only does the author glorify the missionary work of the Society of Jesus above all other religious orders in Peru, he also refers specifically to the Jesuits as "our."[3] From the earliest academic discussions of the text it has been attributed to a particular Jesuit, Blas Valera, by a majority of Andean scholars. González de la Rosa (1907, 1908, 1909), Philip Means, León Lopétegui, Francisco Loaysa, who published an edition of the *Account* under the name of Blas Valera, Alfred Métraux, Enrique Fernández García, and Henrique Urbano have all argued that Valera was the author of this anonymous text.[4]

The text begins with a discussion of religion in the Andes during the Inca Empire and concludes with a description of Christian evangelization in Peru during the first sixty years of Spanish rule. The author praises Inca religious institutions and beliefs in the highest terms possible while presenting harsh criticisms of the Spanish abuse of native peoples. Valera does not spare Catholic missionaries from accusations of mistreating Andean Indians. In fact, he argues that any difficulties in spreading the gospel among native Peruvians were due to the missionaries' own deficiencies, and not to the alleged inability of the Indians to understand the higher truths of Christianity. Valera's Jesuit superior, José de Acosta, had argued that the greatest difficulty for missionaries in the Andes was the "bestial customs" of the Indians, which made it impossible for the latter to accept Christianity. Christianity was inimical to Andean peoples, Acosta stated, because of their low level of morality, the result of living with the customs of animals rather than those of men (Acosta 1954, 409–14). In contrast, Valera asserts that Andean religion provided a solid basis for Christianity. Moreover, he claims that with good instruction and moral examples, native Peruvians could become even better Christians than most Spaniards and therefore deserved full rights and equal treatment within the Spanish kingdom.

In 1594, when the *Account* was written, Valera was in Quito, where he had been transferred in 1593 with the intention that he

---

3. "In this the Dominicans greatly distinguished themselves, and in nothing did they turn away from our spirit and method of proceeding."

4. See the appendix for an extended discussion of the authorship of the text.

would sail to Spain within a few months.[5] However, he fell ill in Quito and his journey was delayed for a year until he recovered. In light of the multiple hands that wrote the original text, he apparently dictated the *Account* to two or three different individuals while bedridden. We know that while in Quito Valera became friends with other Jesuits there who shared some of his pro-Indian views, including Father Hernando Morillo, a Spanish Jesuit, and Father Onofre Esteban.[6]

The *Account* is a more informal work than Valera's lengthy magnum opus, the *Historia occidentalis* (History of the West),[7] which he completed while under house arrest in Lima from 1587 to 1593 (for more on Valera's "crime" and imprisonment, see chapter 2). This shorter work, similar to a modern "position paper," appears to have been intended primarily for dissemination among his fellow Jesuits. It is likely that it was inspired by the recent publication of José de Acosta's *Historia natural y moral de las Indias* (*Natural and Moral History of the Indies*) in Spain in 1590. Acosta, Valera's superior and one of the most powerful Jesuits in Peru, frequently disagreed with Valera on matters such as whether native Peruvian religious customs were harmful and should be allowed within Andean Christianity. Although the *Account* never criticizes Acosta directly, it emphatically disagrees with Acosta on a number of important issues (for more on Acosta and the *Account*, see chapter 3). Valera's defense of Inca religion by equating it with Roman Catholicism, along with his assertion that many contemporary Andean Indians were sincere Christians, were radical ideas in the sixteenth century; it is not surprising that this important text languished unpublished until 1879, when the scholar Marcos Jiménez de la Espada (1879) included it in a volume of texts on the ancient Andes.

Andean Religion Before the Spanish Invasion

Prior to the Spanish conquest of Peru in 1532, Andean peoples worshipped a multitude of sacred beings. Each region of the Inca

5. Valera's departure was mentioned in a letter of December 1594, from Father Hernando Morillo to the Jesuit General, Claudio Aquaviva, printed in *Monumenta peruana* 1966–86, 5:646.

6. Ibid.; Onofre Esteban was from the same town, Chachapoyas, as Valera.

7. For a discussion of the *Historia occidentalis,* see Hyland 2003, 72–76.

Empire revered numerous local deities, such as Llocllay Huancupa in Huarochiri, along with an astonishing variety of other holy beings, including mountain peaks, unusual boulders, and ancestral mummies. The Inca state demanded that all citizens participate in the worship of state deities, such as the sun god (Inti), yet allowed local peoples to retain their own gods, and even expanded the worship of the most important regional deities. As the Jesuit chronicler Bernabe Cobo wrote in 1653, "Although it is true that the Peruvian kings required all conquered persons to receive their Inca religion, they were not required to abandon entirely the religion that they had before" (Cobo 1990, 3).

The two levels of Inca religion—that of the official Inca cults and that of the infinity of local gods—coexisted easily until the Spanish invasion. After the fall of the Inca Empire, the conquistadors successfully destroyed Inca cultic practices yet were relatively helpless against local Andean religion, much of which exists today in a seamless blend with Christian beliefs.[8]

The Inca Pantheon

VIRACOCHA

The mysterious creator known as Viracocha was apparently so holy that he had no official name; instead he was known by different metaphors indicating aspects of his power (Cobo 1990, 22–23). These titles included Pachayachachic (Instructor of Space and Time) and Ticci Viracocha (Divine Origin);[9] Valera's preferred term was Illa Tecce (Eternal Light or Sacred Origin). In one version of the Inca creation story, Viracocha emerged from the waters of Lake Titicaca and created a race of giants whom he later destroyed. Then he called the sun, moon, and stars to come forth from an island in Lake Titicaca and placed these luminaries in the sky. Finally he molded humans out of the stones along the lakeshore (Urton 1999, 34–40). The various Inca creation myths describe Viracocha as a tall man wearing a white garment who gave to each ethnic group its clothes, language,

8. For Spanish attempts to extirpate local Andean religion, see Mills 1997; Griffiths 1996; and Arriaga 1968.
9. *Ticci* is the same as *Tecce* or *Teqsi* and means "origin." *Viracocha,* as defined by Cobo, signifies "divine"; literally it means "sea fat" or, metaphorically, "immense vitality."

songs, and foods. In addition to his temple in Cuzco, Quishuarcancha, he was worshipped at the temple of Raqchi between Cuzco and Lake Titicaca. While no major ceremony was devoted exclusively to him, he was included in the prayers at most major Inca festivals.

The sun, Inti, was a central figure within the official Inca religion. He was the patron of the empire, and his major feast, Inti Raymi, was celebrated during the June solstice. A life-sized golden statue of a boy called Punchao (Day) represented the sun god within the central temple—the Coricancha—in Cuzco. After the death of each Inca emperor, the king's internal organs were burned and the ashes placed inside Punchao's hollow belly, emphasizing the sacred link between the sun god and the Inca royalty.

The *Vilahoma*, the high priest who presided over the sun worship in Coricancha, always came from the royal Inca Tarpuntae lineage (Cobo 1990, 158). He was assisted by female *acllas*, consecrated virgins who lived in the *acllahuasi* (house of the chosen women), next door to the Coricancha. The *acllas* cooked special food to serve to Punchao and the other idols in the temple; they cared for the sacred fire in Coricancha; and they wove very fine cloth for statues of the gods and for the Inca nobility. Throughout the empire, the Incas built numerous sun temples with the accompanying enclosures for *acllas;* these were always among the finest Inca buildings in the provinces.

The moon, Mama Quilla, was the wife of the sun and the patroness of women in the empire. A life-sized statue of a woman represented the moon goddess in Coricancha. She was served by her own priestesses, who offered her food and other sacrifices, wove beautiful clothing for her, and carried her statue in religious processions in Cuzco (Cobo 1990, 29). A major temple to the moon existed on the Island of the Moon in Lake Titicaca (Bauer and Stanish 2001, 98–131). Pilgrims came to this temple from all over the empire to worship the image of the moon, a life-sized statue of a woman, gold from the waist up and silver from the waist down.

The thunder god, Illapa, was depicted in mythology as a man in the sky, wielding a war club in one hand and a sling in the other. The thunder was the crack of his sling, while the lightning was the flash of his golden garments as he raced through the sky. Andean people prayed to him for rain that he drew from the Milky Way, believed to be a river in the sky. The Incas maintained a major shrine to Illapa in a temple called Pukamarka in Cuzco (Bauer 1998, 58).

OTHER HOLY BEINGS: *HUACAS*

The concept of the *huaca* is central to an understanding of Andean religiosity, both in Inca times and today. A *huaca* is any material manifestation of the superhuman; it can be found in a mountain peak, a spring, a union of rivers, a cave, a rock outcrop, and "any number of humanly made objects in shrines: effigies, human mummies, oracles, and so forth" (Salomon 1991, 16). Local *huacas* ranged in importance from major oracles and deities to small carved stones that were believed to protect a household. Major regional *huacas* such as Llocllay Huancupa had permanent priesthoods and even, on occasion, human wives.

According to one seventeenth-century source, local people addressed their major *huaca* as *runap camac* (creator of men and women; Arriaga 1968, 50). It is important to note that the Andean idea of creation in the verb *camay* does not mean to create out of nothing; rather, it "connotes the energizing of extant matter . . . a continuous act that works upon a being as long as it exists" (Salomon 1991, 16). Humans are "created" by their *huaca* of origin in the sense that the *huaca* infused vitality and identity into them and continues to do so. Thus, humans need to give offerings and sacrifices to the *huaca* as a form of reciprocity for the continuing energy given them by the *huaca*. Different animal species often have constellations as their *camac* or creator.[10] For example, the Yacana constellation, in the shape of a llama, "infuses a powerful generative essence of llama vitality, which causes earthly llamas to flourish" (Salomon 1991, 16). The *camac* of a human group was usually its *huaca* of origin, the subject of myths and legends that revealed the *huaca*'s individual personality. In the *Account*, Valera attributes the *huaca*'s vitalizing power to its ultimate source, the creator Viracocha, while defining *huaca* more narrowly as a shrine, a sacred cavern, or a grave. His emphasis on the central role of the creator in Andean belief, rather

---

10. In the Andes, constellations are often "dark cloud constellations"; that is, they are the areas of dark gas clouds surrounded by stars. See Urton 1981, 169–91.

than on the local *huacas*, helps to underscore one of his central themes—the similarity between ancient Peruvian religion and Christianity.

Rituals

The *Account* does not discuss major annual festivals such as Inti Raymi, the sun celebration held during the June solstice. Instead, Valera focuses on more personal religious rituals like confession and burials.

CONFESSION

The private, oral confession of one's sins to a priest was a central ritual in the pre-Columbian Andes. Each person had to confess his or her sins at least once a year, usually in June (MacCormack 1991, 421). Because it was thought that hidden sins caused illness and misfortune to the community, private confession was a public duty. Women often confessed to female priestesses, who performed other sacred tasks, such as making the beer used in sacrifices and keeping the ceremonial clothes of the *huacas* (423).

Confession usually took place near a river so that the penitent could symbolically cast away his or her sins afterwards. During the ritual the confessor often threw lots or performed other auguries to determine if the penitent had revealed all of his or her sins. If not, the confessor would beat the penitent on the back with a small stone, and the confession would resume. Andean confessions were still common at the time Valera penned the *Account;* as one chronicler wrote, Andean people still "eat *hichu*, which is a kind of grass, and spit it out, declaring their sins to sorcerers" (Martín de Murúa, in Mac-Cormack 1991, 202). Penances included fasting, being whipped with nettles, or, in more severe cases, a period of exile in the wilderness. In the *Account*, Valera explains that some individuals chose voluntarily to live a life of penance in the wilderness as a type of hermit; the local villagers looked to these individuals for help in practical matters, such as prayers for a healthy birth. In the sixteenth century, Augustinian friars in northern Peru actually encountered one such non-Christian Andean hermit living in the wilderness as penance for his sins (*Relación de idolatrías* 1918, 43).

Written Spanish sources disagree about the nature of the sins confessed by Andean peoples. Writers who considered Andean religion
to be demonic and corrupt claimed that Andeans confessed only to
exterior acts, and not to sinful thoughts (Cobo 1990, 122). However,
writers such as Valera, who viewed Andean practices more positively,
stated that Andeans confessed to "evil desires" as well as to exterior acts of sin. This contradiction reflects contemporary European
debates over exterior versus interior forms of worship, in which
many theologians viewed interior sentiment and consent to God as
more worthy than exterior acts of devotion (see MacCormack 1991,
347). Thus, apologists for the Incas, like Valera, argued that Andean
peoples shared a similar concern over one's interior disposition and
confessed to sinful thoughts as well as to sinful deeds.

BURIALS AND MUMMIFICATION

Burial practices throughout the Andes varied enormously from
region to region. Sadly, the conquistadors and their successors were
so successful at looting and destroying elite Inca tombs that virtually
none remain today (D'Altroy 2002, 194). Spanish chroniclers tell us
that Andean peoples built tombs both under and above the ground,
although the latter were more common (Cobo 1990, 24649). Yet
whatever the tomb style, its size and elaborateness depended upon
the status of the deceased.

The bodies of individuals who were powerful when alive were
intentionally preserved after death. The mummies of these important
lords, dressed in the finest clothing, were placed in their tombs with
most of their personal property, including dishes of gold and silver
(Cobo 1990, 39–43). Wives and servants who wished to accompany
their lord into the afterlife—a great honor—asked to be strangled
during a ceremony in which they drank large amounts of alcohol
and lamented their fallen leader. At major festivals, the mummies
of the lords, newly dressed, were brought out and given food and
other offerings. Special priests, able to communicate with the dead,
served the mummies and spoke for them. Andean peoples clearly
believed that the dead were still with us and that the dividing line
between life and death was more porous than we usually acknowl-
edge. Andean peoples thought that if they honored and gave gifts
to the deceased ancestors, their own prosperity and progeny would

increase. Although Valera notes that the dead were treated with great reverence, he is careful to argue that they were never worshipped themselves; in this he is offering an interpretation of the Andean mummy cults that conforms to Christian ideals of the proper objects of worship.

Religious Universals in the Sixteenth and Seventeenth Centuries

In addition to presenting important information about religion in the Andes, *Account of the Ancient Customs* is an early example of a text that implicitly looks for religious universals through finding similarities between Christian and non-Christian religions. Today works such as *Christ the Eternal Tao* (Damascene 2004), *Jesus and Lao Tzu: The Parallel Sayings* (Aronson 2002), and *Living Buddha, Living Christ* (Hanh 1995) abound, generated by the public's interest in understanding the commonalities underlying Christianity and the great religious traditions of Asia. In the sixteenth and seventeenth centuries, there existed writers, such as Valera, who felt compelled to understand the ways in which indigenous religions shared essential features with Christianity. However, such writers were in the minority and were often forced to suffer for their beliefs.

The Italian Jesuits Matteo Ricci (1552–1610) and Roberto de Nobili (1577–1656) were the two most famous advocates of the attitude that today would be referred to as "inculturation," that is, the acceptance of indigenous "religious" customs within Christianity. In China, Ricci dressed in the robes of a Confucian scholar and argued that Chinese converts to Christianity should be allowed to practice traditional rites such as ancestor worship (Cronin 1955; Minamiki 1985). Ricci's ideas on inculturation were extremely controversial. His opponents argued that Ricci's three main innovations—using the Chinese word for God, allowing Chinese Christians to participate in rites for Confucius, and allowing Christians to perform Chinese ancestor rites—were idolatrous and perverse. This dispute was not settled until 1705, when Pope Clement XVI forbade all of Ricci's innovations (Minamiki 1985).

In India, several years after Ricci, his confrere De Nobili adopted the saffron dress, wooden clogs, and vegetarian diet of a Brahmin holy man. Like Ricci, De Nobili allowed converts to retain native customs such as, in this case, marking the brow, wearing the Brahmin thread, and making ceremonial ablutions. De Nobili even went so far as to write sacred texts on palm leaves like a Brahmin pundit and to try to replace Latin with Sanskrit in the seminary (Cronin 1959). He also advocated using Sanskrit terms to describe Christian ideas. Yet for his efforts in inculturation he was persecuted by the leading Portuguese Jesuits; he was twice censored and for many years was forbidden from any missionary activity whatsoever. Had he not been the nephew of Robert Bellarmine, the most powerful cardinal in Italy, his punishment would likely have been more severe. The debate about whether his form of inculturation was heretical was so controversial it finally had to be decided by the pope. Only in 1623, with the timely intervention of a new pontiff, Gregory XV, was De Nobili allowed to continue his radical missionary methods.[11]

Although Valera, Ricci, and De Nobili were all Jesuits, it is unlikely that the other two were acquainted with Valera's writings, which were suppressed by the Spanish Jesuits. Yet this very brief summary of the missionary ideals of Ricci and De Nobili can help to contextualize Valera's writing and struggles. Like Ricci and De Nobili, Valera sought to integrate indigenous custom and thought into Christianity, and, like their experiments with inculturation, his evoked a harsh, negative reaction (described in chapter 2).

De Nobili and Ricci both wrote highly controversial works expounding the similarities between Christianity and the native faiths—Vedantic Hinduisim and Confucianism, respectively—they

---

11. Most scholars believe that De Nobili is the author of the famous "fifth Veda" or pseudo-Veda. De Nobili is known to have written that, while the Hindus have four Vedas, there existed another Veda, one preached by Jesus Christ, which De Nobili would teach to anyone who wished to learn it. In the eighteenth century, Voltaire acquired the French translation of a Sanskrit Veda that combined Christian and Hindu ideas to espouse a Hindu version of Christianity. Although Voltaire believed this Veda to be authentic, in 1822 Francis Whyte Ellis convincingly argued that it had been written by De Nobili. Through analyzing the text's content and language, he proved that an early Jesuit missionary, one well versed in Sanskrit and Brahmanic thought, had written it. When Ellis showed the text to the Christian Indians of Pondicherry, they recognized it from their oral traditions and told him that De Nobili had composed it. Although most experts have been convinced by the general thrust of Ellis's arguments, there has been considerable controversy over whether De Nobili forged the Veda himself, whether a follower of De Nobili formed the Veda out of extracts from De Nobili's writings (Ellis's opinion), or whether the entire Veda was written by one of De Nobili's Jesuit followers (Rocher 1984, 19–34).

encountered. Although *Account of the Ancient Customs* shares a similar spirit with their writings, it has never received the same attention. Yet with its unique insights into Inca religious traditions and the missionary controversies over inculturation, this text offers considerable scope for studying religion and culture in the Andean world and beyond. The *Account* is important too for revealing a sample of the diversity of opinion in sixteenth-century Spanish America about "Indian" religion. All too often English-speaking readers can have an unexamined prejudice that Spanish thinking in Peru was simply lockstep obedience to the Spanish Inquisition. This text shows that there also existed pro-Indian voices at this time, the dawn of Euro-American history from 1518 to 1625, whose ideals of natural rights paved the way for the Enlightenment and more recent human rights formulations (see Tierney 1997).

2

Blas Valera: His Life and "Crimes"

Early Years

The birthplace of Blas Valera can be found in the high-altitude
jungles of Chachapoyas, a relatively remote area in northern Peru
known as the "cloud forest." Chachapoyas, home to an important
pre-Inca civilization, is a land of great natural beauty, with steep,
craggy mountains, fast-moving rivers, and thick, tropical forests
made up of low trees, mosses, ferns, and wild orchids. Yet the same
features that contributed to the region's charms also helped to isolate
the area from the rest of Spanish Peru. The mountains, rivers, and
dense vegetation hindered travel and trade between Chachapoyas and
the major Spanish settlements in the highlands and along the coast.
The climate—one of the rainiest on earth—also made Chachapoyas
less attractive to Spanish settlers. During the rainy season, from September to March, Chachapoyas receives daily inundations of fog and
rain; during the dry season, snowstorms, freezing rain, and hail can
occur in the higher elevations.

Luis Valera, Blas's father according to the Jesuit Provincial
Catalogues (*Monumenta peruana* 1966–86, 1:284), was a leading
landowner and rancher in the Spanish community of Chachapoyas.
Born in the mountains of western Andalusia, Luis left Spain for the
Indies in 1534 (Bermudez Plata 1944, 304), arriving in Peru soon
after Francisco Pizarro's capture and execution of the Inca emperor
Atahuallpa. Fortunately for Luis, his kinsman, Francisco de Chaves,
was one of Pizarro's most trusted friends and companions. It is
likely that Luis fought on Pizarro's side in the 1537 civil war against
Diego de Almagro. Certainly by 1538 Luis had signed on as a captain
under the command of Alonso de Alvarado in the Spanish expedition against Chachapoyas. Upon the successful completion of the
Spaniards' military campaign, Alvarado rewarded Luis richly for his

service, granting Luis the *encomiendas* (grants of free native labor tribute) of Chibalta and Tiapullu (Alvarado 1965, 159; Puente Brunke 1992, 479, 484). Luis built his country estate in the town of Quitaya, where it is likely his son Blas was born. Like the other *encomenderos* of northern Chachapoyas, Luis would have raised livestock, including cattle, llamas, goats, horses, and mules. His estate produced salt, one of the region's most lucrative industries. Gold was also an important product of Chachapoyas, and Luis undoubtedly made his native workers pan for gold in the local streams and rivers. Luis spent part of every year in his Inca house in the city of Chachapoyas, about twenty miles south of Quitaya. There he served as a prominent member of the city council, eventually being elected judge and royal treasurer (Hyland 2003, 15–20).

Little is known about Blas Valera's mother, an Indian woman named Francisca Perez (*Monumenta peruana* 1966–86, 1:284), according to the Jesuit Provincial Catalogue. Several scholars have speculated that she was an Inca noblewoman from the court of Atahuallpa (Esteve Barba 1966, xliii; González de la Rosa 1907, 190). Although there is no solid evidence, it seems almost certain that she was of Inca, rather than Chachapoyan, descent. The language she taught Blas was Quechua, an Inca tongue, not Chachapoyan, suggesting strongly she was Inca. Her son Blas was highly biased in favor of the Incas, at the expense of other native groups in South America (see, for example, Valera, cited in Garcilaso de la Vega 1987, 261–64, 393–95). He was also strongly partisan in favor of Atahuallpa against Atahuallpa's brother and rival for the throne, Huascar (see Valera, cited by Anello Oliva 1998, 107–8). Although Francisca never married Luis, she lived on his estate and appears to have given birth to at least one other son, Jerónimo, who would become a leading Franciscan writer in Peru (Hyland 2003, 22–27).

In 1559, when Blas was fifteen years old, his Spanish stepmother, Catalina Rodríguez de Aldana, Luis Valera's legitimate wife whom he had left behind in Spain twenty-five years earlier, joined the Valera household in Chachapoyas (Bermudez Plata 1944, 324). Yet Blas would not remain for long in the household run by his stepmother; Luis eventually sent Blas to the northern coastal city of Trujillo, where the young man studied Latin, theology, and the liberal arts (*Monumenta peruana* 1966–86, 2:141). According to Garcilaso's citations from Valera, Blas devoted many hours in Trujillo to talking to the *amautas*—historians and storytellers—of Atahuallpa. From these men he learned firsthand about the legends of the Inca's northern court in Quito. After completing his studies in Trujillo, Blas chose to become a member of the Society of Jesus rather than return home permanently to his father's and stepmother's household in Chachapoyas.

Life as a Jesuit

When Valera joined the Society of Jesus in Lima on November 29, 1568, the Jesuits had been in Peru for only six months, having arrived in April 1568 (*Monumenta peruana* 1966–86, 2:141). The other religious communities—the Franciscans, Dominicans, Mercedarians, and Augustinians—already had been established in Peru for many years, with their own parishes, mission territories, and patrons. The Jesuits had been founded by Saint Ignatius Loyola only twenty-eight years earlier,[1] and in Spain, during the early decades of their existence, they had to compete for patronage and resources with older and better-established religious orders and institutions. Although today the Jesuits may seem to have been an integral aspect of the early modern Church, in the sixteenth century their survival was not at all assured. In fact, in the later decades of the century the Spanish Crown and the Spanish Inquisition came close to destroying the fledgling order. Philip II of Spain worked fervently to bring the Spanish Jesuits under his personal supervision for the stated goal of enforcing religious and political orthodoxy (Lopétegui 1942; *New Catholic Encyclopedia*, 1st ed., s.v. "Aquaviva, Claudius"). Although Philip ultimately was unable to assert that level of control, the Jesuit leadership was forced to take extreme care not to give the Spanish Crown any excuse for subsuming the Society.

Likewise, the Spanish Inquisition resented the privileges granted to the newly founded Society and tried to suppress it. For example, in the 1580s, the inquisitors of Valladolid imprisoned a Jesuit theologian on trumped-up charges of heresy and attempted to use these

---

1. The Jesuits were so new in the sixteenth century that they were sometimes confused with the Theatines, another new Roman Catholic religious order at the time. Valera refers to this confusion in the final section of the *Account*, where he has the Jesuits' critics call the Society "Theatines" rather than "Jesuits."

accusations as an excuse for driving the Jesuits out of Spain (Courson 1879, 159–60). In reaction to these threats, the Jesuit leadership in the Spanish Empire strongly discouraged their members from any theological or political discussions that even remotely suggested heresy or criticism of the Spanish Crown. By the late 1570s, the Jesuit General specifically and repeatedly instructed the Jesuits in Peru to refrain from any activities that would provide the Crown with a reason to remove the Jesuits from their South American missions (for the text of these letters, see *Monumenta peruana* 1966–86, 2:477–78, 565). As a result of this policy, the writings of at least two Jesuits in Peru— José de Acosta and Giovanni Anello Oliva—were heavily censored to eliminate any criticisms of Spanish activities in the New World from their texts (Hyland 2003, 176–82, 229–32).

As we shall see, the ever-tightening restrictions on expression by Jesuit priests in the later sixteenth century would bode ill for Valera, who ultimately would be imprisoned by the Jesuits themselves under the charge of heresy. However, none of this was apparent yet in the early days of the Jesuit missions in Peru. As a novice, Valera was singled out for praise in the Jesuit Annual Letter of 1569, which stated, "[Valera] is a great Latinist and poet and a great linguist in many languages here, which was what we greatly desired so that we go forward in learning the [languages] spoken here" (*Monumenta peruana* 1966–86, 1:266; my translation). The early Jesuits in Peru believed that men of mixed Indian and Spanish ancestry, like Valera, would make ideal missionaries because they would be rooted in the Christianity of their European fathers while fluent in their mothers' native languages (Hyland 1998). As an outstanding linguist, Valera certainly fulfilled their expectations in this regard.

By 1570, Valera's novitiate was over, and he professed his first vows. Soon after this, he was sent to be part of the Jesuits' first stable mission in Peru in Huarochiri. Years later an Italian Jesuit, Giovanni Anello Oliva, praised Valera's work in Huarochiri:

> Because of being a mestizo—son of a Spanish father and his mother an Indian—he knew the language of the land with the perfection of the selfsame Indians, which was very important and very useful for this ministry, because as the Indians saw that this missionary possessed as large a portion of their blood and ethnicity as he did of the Spanish, they believed what he

told them; they paid more attention to his words than to those of another. It seemed to them that if he did not believe his words to be true, he would not have preached them, nor, even less, would he, being of their lineage, deceive them. (Anello Oliva 1998, 254; my translation. Most of this quote in praise of Valera was crossed out by Jesuit censors.)

Despite Valera's apparent successes in Huarochiri, the Jesuits decided to abandon the Huarochiri mission in 1572 (Hyland 2003, 38–47). Valera's next assignment was in Santiago del Cercado, a native parish for Indians located on the outskirts of Lima. In 1573, while Valera was in El Cercado, he was ordained as a priest, the first mestizo Jesuit to receive holy orders in South America (*Monumenta peruana* 1966–86, 1:706). After serving satisfactorily for several years in El Cercado, he was transferred to the Jesuit house in Cuzco, the ancient Inca capital (*Monumenta peruana* 1966–86, 2:140–41). In Cuzco he taught Latin and preached to and heard confessions from natives. He was also the spiritual advisor for the Indian Nombre de Jesús confraternity, whose membership included many important Inca nobles. Every Wednesday and Friday the confraternity met for "spiritual discussions" led by Valera. It may have been at these meetings that Valera began to develop and refine his radical views concerning the Inca and Christian religions.

However, by 1576, the Society decided to transfer Valera to the city of Potosí. In response, the "Indians of Cuzco" staged massive public protests in the city, passing one day and night crying outside the Jesuit College and then marching through the streets the next day, shouting and shedding more tears. As a leading Jesuit, José de Acosta, explained, "There came to the Father Visitor and me an infinity of Indians, bringing us a written petition and asking us with great sentiment that we not take from them Father Valera, by whose means they knew God and were Christians; and not content with this, they went to the house of the Spanish administrator of this city and they gave such an outcry that they made him come another turn with them and the other Spaniards about the same demand" (published in *Monumenta peruana* 1966–86, 2:269–70).

Because of the native protests, Valera's transfer to Potosí was delayed. Nonetheless, by 1577 he had been sent to the native parish of Juli in southern Peru. After serving in Juli for two years, he was then moved to the Potosí, the silver-mining capital of South America. It should be noted that it was normal for Jesuit missionaries to be transferred frequently; the mobility that was a part of the Jesuit spirit demanded that its members not become too accustomed to any one parish. In Potosí Valera apparently founded a new native confraternity (Hyland 2003, 52–63) and continued his researches into native culture and beliefs.

Finally, in 1582, he was recalled to Lima to work on translating the new Catholic catechism that had been ordered by the Third Lima Council of Bishops. In Lima he offered free Quechua classes to anyone, priest or layperson, who wished to learn the language (AGI 1583). Valera was also responsible for preparing the Aymara translation of the catechism. Throughout this work, he used native terms for Christian ecclesiastical concepts like "God," "priest," and "chastity" (Bartra 1967). This was in marked contrast to the policy of most members of the translation committee, who favored using Spanish terms for religious ideas; they believed that Andean values and beliefs were too corrupt to have any place in Christianity, and so, therefore, native religious terms should not be used in a Christian text. The widely disseminated Quechua translation of the catechism scrupulously avoided using native religious terms (Hyland 2003, 64–69).

By late in the year 1582, Valera had completed the Aymara translation and was looking forward to being transferred back to Potosí. However, on December 14 of that year, in a move that must have alarmed Valera, the leading Jesuits in Peru voted unanimously to forbid the acceptance of any more men of Indian descent into the Society; as their decision stated, they agreed to "close the door to mestizos . . . because experience has shown at length that this class of people does not do well" (*Monumenta peruana* 1966–86, 3:205–6; my translation). One of the Jesuits who voted for this decision later explained that it was necessary because of the "notable pain" caused by the crimes of Blas Valera (*Monumenta peruana* 1966–86, 3:547–50). In fact, by April of 1583, Valera was incarcerated in an underground prison cell in the Jesuit house in Lima, charged with a mysterious crime. When the Jesuit procurator for the Peruvian province left for Europe on April 11, 1583, part of his mission was to explain to the Jesuit general in person why Valera ought to be dismissed from the Society. This information had to be communicated personally, it was stated, because the Valera affair was too sensitive to commit to paper (*Monumenta peruana* 1966–86, 3:675).

The Jesuit scholar Rubén Vargas Ugarte has stated unequivocally that Valera was a prisoner of the Inquisition, incarcerated for fornication with a woman (Vargas Ugarte 1963, 251). Yet an Italian Jesuit who had been in Peru, Lucio Garcete, testified before the Panama Inquisition in 1591 that, while the Jesuits claimed that Valera had been imprisoned by the Inquisition, this was not the case (Garcete 2003, 244). Rather, he said, the Jesuits themselves had incarcerated Valera.[2] In fact, a survey of the Inquisition records from Peru between 1582 and 1598 reveals no mention of Valera whatsoever. In general, each case tried by the Inquisition lasted several years, and so each case is mentioned repeatedly in each yearly report; if Valera had been tried by the Inquisition, his case would have been found at least once among the Inquisition records.

Valera's case also differs markedly from that of the two Jesuits in Peru who were convicted by the Inquisition of fornication. In the early 1580s, both Miguel de Fuentes and Luis López ran afoul of the Lima inquisitors on charges of seducing and raping young women. Both of these cases, it should be noted, were discussed in the correspondence between the Jesuits in Peru and in Rome, unlike Valera's situation, which was too delicate to mention. Fuentes was found guilty of seducing most of the young nuns in the convent of La Concepción in Lima, along with a group of laywomen. For his crimes, the Holy Office sentenced him to be reprimanded in front of his superiors in the Lima house and to be forbidden from confessing women for ten years (AHN n.d.b; 1580–81b; 1581–82a). López was convicted by the Inquisition of the brutal rape of several young women in Lima, including the mentally unbalanced Doña María Pizarro, injuring the latter so severely in his attack that she was forced to seek medical treatment. Inquisitors also found among his papers a single heretical statement that "God wanted our first pontiff Saint Peter to be first tempted and to fall into temptation." For his crimes of rape and one count of heresy he was ordered to return to Spain, where

---

2. The Jesuit house in Lima rented out prison cells to the Spanish Inquisition during the late 1500s. This practice began when the Inquisitors asked the Jesuits to house some captured English pirates, and later became customary. Jesuit superiors, therefore, would have been able to maintain plausibly that any prisoner in their house, such as Valera, was a charge of the Holy Office (AHN 1580a; AHN 1595).

he was to endure two years of house arrest and never again confess women (AHN 1580–81a; 1581–82a). Nothing was added to these sentences by the Jesuits themselves.

Valera's punishment, which was decided by the Jesuit General in Rome, Claudio Acquaviva, and by the Peruvian provincial, and not by the Inquisitors, was much more severe (*Monumenta peruana* 1966–86, 4:302–3). Sentenced to spend four years in an underground prison cell in the Jesuit house in Lima, he was forced to fast, pray, and practice weekly "mortifications," which consisted of floggings under the supervision of the provincial. Valera's formerly good health appears to have broken down under this harsh regime, and he would be plagued by illness for the rest of his life. After the four years of incarceration, he was offered the opportunity to leave the Jesuits and join another religious order. Maintaining his innocence of any wrongdoing, he refused to leave the Society and, under the terms of his initial sentence, was put under house arrest in Lima for six years, from 1587 to 1593. During this time he was not allowed to perform any of the sacramental functions of a priest, talk to outsiders, or leave the house for any reason. He was also required to perform only "low offices," such as cleaning and tending to the sick.

While it seems clear that, as Garcete stated, Valera was imprisoned by the Jesuits and not by the Inquisition, what was his crime—so sensitive that it could not be described on paper, and merited such a harsh punishment? In his 1591 testimony, Garcete suggested that Valera's imprisonment was inspired by fear of the Inquisition when the Peruvian superiors learned of the imprisonment of Jesuits in Valladolid on trumped-up charges of heresy (as Garcete stated, "when they learned of the imprisonment of our men in Valladolid by order of the Most Illustrious Lord Cardinal of Toledo, the Head Inquisitor"; my translation); this occurred as the Inquisition looked for any excuse of heresy to expel the Jesuits from Spain (Garcete 2003, 244). Moreover, Garcete specified that Valera's imprisonment by the Jesuits was under the privilege that the Jesuits enjoyed of dealing specifically with cases of heresy among their members on their own, without recourse to the Inquisition. The Jesuits in Peru received this privilege, granted to them by the Roman Curia, in the spring of 1583 (Yale 1508–1634, fol. 3b) when the flotilla arrived; Valera was imprisoned immediately afterwards. Prior to the granting of this privilege, any Jesuit suspected of heresy had to be turned over to the Holy Office.

This privilege applied only to cases of heresy; its use in the case of Valera reveals that his "crime" was one of suspected heresy.

Unfortunately, Jesuit documents do not discuss any details of what Valera's heretical views may have been. However, we can gain insights into his "crime" by looking at the details of his punishment. As we saw, the two Jesuits convicted of fornication and rape were forbidden from confessing women. What was Valera forbidden from ever doing again, even after he served his time? General Acquaviva (*Monumenta peruana* 1966–86, 6:168–69), who knew the entire story of Valera's misdeeds, insisted vehemently that Valera never again be allowed to teach grammar; that is, Quechua and Aymara. It appears that Valera's "heresy" was somehow tied to the Quechua classes he gave for free in Lima and to his work of translation into Aymara; these issues of grammar, politics, and heresy will be explored later in this chapter.

It should be noted that Valera was not the only Jesuit in Peru imprisoned by order of the Jesuit General Acquaviva for having radical ideals. Martín de Funes, a Spanish Jesuit who wanted to found a utopian pro-Indian missionary community in Peru, was likewise condemned by Acquaviva (Piras 2006). Criticizing the mistreatment of Indians by Spanish *encomenderos* (owners of a grant of free labor from Indians), and unhappy with current missionary efforts, Funes argued for founding a utopian community modeled on the primitive Church. In this community, made up of both religious and lay people, there would be total poverty and natives would be protected and treated with respect. On October 24, 1609, when Acquaviva found out that Funes had communicated his ideas to the pope, the general branded Funes an "apostate" and ordered him imprisoned immediately. With the help of influential friends, Funes was able to escape; he died a year and a half later while still evading capture.

During his period in prison, Valera had written to the Jesuit General in Rome, requesting a transfer to Europe because of his failing health (*Monumenta peruana* 1966–86, 4:189). While Valera was under house arrest, General Acquaviva considered the matter, stating that his own preference, however, was for Valera to leave the Jesuits and join a mendicant order in Peru. Valera's provincial, José de Acosta, argued that Valera should be transferred to Europe "because of the danger of doing harm to others and of receiving harm himself" if he remained in Peru (Hyland 2003, 190–91). Eventually, Acosta's reasoning carried the day, and in 1593 Valera was transferred to Quito with the intention that he would sail for Spain the following year. However, he fell ill in Quito and his journey was delayed until 1595. In May 1596 he arrived in Spain, where he was sent to the city of Cádiz and placed under the care of Cristóbal Méndez, the provincial of Andalusia, who was ordered to keep Valera locked up until further notice.

Valera's stay in Cádiz was doomed to be brief. Several months after he arrived there, the English lord Robert Devereux, earl of Essex, sacked the city. According to eyewitness accounts, the Protestant Devereux and his men roamed the streets, searching for and beating any Catholic priest whom they found. Valera, whose health was already weak, was badly injured in the violent attack and was removed to Malagá, where he died on April 2 of 1597. The modern scholar José Durand found Valera listed among those who died in the College of Malagá in 1597, according to the handwritten necrology in the archives of the Jesuit province of Toledo (Durand 1987). Valera was fifty-three years old at the time of his death.

It was while under house arrest that Valera appears to have written his greatest work, the *Historia Occidentalis,* consisting of at least five books, each one having multiple chapters (Sandoval 1647, 458). Although most of this work was lost in the English attack on Cádiz, the Peruvian writer Garcilaso de la Vega was able to acquire the remains, which he incorporated into his work the *Royal Commentaries of the Incas.* Garcilaso stated that Valera's book was "a history of the Peruvian empire," and many of the passages by Valera found in Garcilaso discuss Inca religion, government, and language with admiration, while condemning the Spanish conquest of the Inca Empire (Garcilaso de la Vega 1987). As Garcilaso wrote, "I received the remains of the papers which were saved from the pillage, and they caused me great regret and pain at the loss of the rest, the importance of which can be deduced from what survived. What is missing is the greater and better part" (19).

Prior to this work, Valera wrote an account of the conversion of the Andean people to Christianity, completed by 1579 (now lost); he wrote this book while serving in the Jesuit mission of Juli (*Monumenta peruana* 1966–86, 2:812–13). Valera would return to the topic of the Christianization of the Andes in his *Account of the Ancient Customs of the Natives of Peru*, the work translated into English here. As one can observe, the second half of this text focuses on an analysis of the phases of Christian evangelization in the Andes. This work was composed in 1594, toward the end of the author's life, while he lay recuperating in Quito. Additionally, Valera is known to have written a vocabulary in which he explained Quechua terms and names in Spanish. This work has also been lost; however, the Jesuit Giovanni Anello Oliva found a copy in the Jesuit house in La Paz and preserved some citations from it in his manuscript "Lives of Men Famous for Their Sanctity in the Society of Jesus in Peru" (Anello Oliva 1998, 95). These brief quotations reveal that the vocabulary was more like an encyclopedia, providing lengthy entries about the Inca kings and other topics. Within these citations one finds criticisms of the Spanish similar to those in the Valera sections of Garcilaso. For example, referring to the execution of the Inca emperor Atahuallpa at the hands of Pizarro, Valera wrote, "Atahuallpa, the last Inca king of Peru, who was tyrannically and unjustly killed by the tyrant Francisco Pizarro" (Anello Oliva 1998, 138; my translation).

Most curiously, the story of Valera's life and writings does not end with his death in Malagá in 1597. In 1899, a catalogue of the personal library of Emilio di Tommasi, the Italian consul in Bolivia, was published (Cantú 2002, 325–28). According to this publication, among the manuscripts owned by the consul was a notebook entitled *Exsul immeritus Blas Valera populo suo*; a work in Latin, Spanish and cipher called "Historia et Rudimenta Linguae Piruanorum"; a letter by Francisco de Chaves; a multicolored *khipu* (an Inca record-keeping device made of knotted string); and several manuscripts containing drawings of *khipus* and other painted figures. These documents passed into the collection of the Savoya-Aosta family (Laurencich Minelli 2005, 120–22). On November 11, 1927, Amadeo de Saboya, duke of Aosta, gave the documents to Mayor Riccardo Cera as a wedding gift; in 1952, the journalist G. Nardi published a description of the documents in Cera's collection, explaining that Cera liked to show the documents to dinner guests at his house (Nardi 1952). Upon Cera's death in 1958, the documents were passed on to his niece, Clara Miccinelli, the current owner.

Although these documents (referred to in the literature as either the "Naples documents" or the "Miccinelli documents") are too complex to describe here fully, the story of Blas Valera lies at their heart.[3]

---

3. The documents have been published in their entirety in Laurencich Minelli 2005.

They allege that Valera's death in 1597 was faked by Jesuits who wanted to remove him from the Society. After 1597, the texts continue, Valera returned secretly to Peru, where he authored the *New Chronicle and Good Government*, a massive chronicle of Andean life attributed to an Indian, Guaman Poma de Ayala; he is also said to have written and signed at least one of the texts in this collection of documents, the *Exsul Immeritus*. Additionally, the documents state that Valera taught a secret, phonetic *khipu* writing system to his followers, along with a very Andeanized version of Christianity. Moreover, they describe the resistance that Valera encountered among the Jesuits in Peru because of his pro-Indian politics, and argue that these politics were the cause of his imprisonment and exile. The paper and ink of most of this material has been dated to the early seventeenth century (Zoppi 2001; Gasparotto, 2001; Bertoluzza et al. 2001).[4]

For various reasons, such as that Valera's signature on these documents does not match his real signature, many scholars suspect that

4. Some scholars have proposed that the Naples documents are recent forgeries by Miccinelli and others, based on alleged modern anachronisms in the text (Estenssoro 1997; Adorno 1998). Although the supposed anachronisms have been shown not to be modern (Hyland 2003, 214–36), Jeremy Mumford (2000) has argued that this is irrelevant; the negative reputation of the documents' owner suffices to prove that they are modern forgeries. Mumford is referring to ten years of unsubstantiated rumors, spread via the Internet and at conferences, to the effect that the owner of the documents, Clara Miccinelli, is a known forger. This tale first appeared on the Internet in October 1999, when it was erroneously claimed that Miccinelli had been convicted of forgery; the story has grown in the telling since then. The truth behind these rumors is the following.

In the 1750s, Raimondi de Sangro, the prince of Sansevero, who is an ancestor of Clara Miccinelli, rebuilt a chapel in Naples that today is a major tourist attraction. In the 1980s, the owner of the chapel advertised the site to tourists by claiming that Sansevero had created three of the life-sized statues in the chapel from living human beings. Fantastically, it was asserted that Sansevero had injected living people with a mysterious substance that "mineralized" their bodies, killing them instantly, and creating the statues of the two "anatomical machines" (bodies showing the entire circulatory system) and *The Veiled Christ*, one of the great art treasures of Naples. In 1982, in the Naples state archives, Miccinelli found the contract between Sansevero and the sculptor Giuseppe Sanmartino in which the prince paid the artist for sculpting *The Veiled Christ* (Miccinelli 1982). The chapel owner, afraid of losing tourist revenues if the true, mundane origin of the statue were revealed, took Miccinelli to court, alleging that she had forged the contract. However, the judge, appalled at the absurdity of the plaintiff's claims, fully exonerated Miccinelli. Unless one is prepared to believe that Sansevero was the equivalent of Vincent Price's Professor Henry Jarrod in the horror film *House of Wax*, turning beautiful women into wax statues, there is no reason to suspect Miccinelli of forgery.

Recently it has been revealed that the two "anatomical machines" are actually human skeletons covered by an elaborate network of beeswax, iron wire, and silk to mimic arteries and veins (Peters n.d.) and not "vitrified" humans.

the story told by these documents is false, or at least only partially true. I have argued elsewhere that the most reasonable explanation for these texts is that they were written secretly by Jesuits in Peru who wished to carry on Valera's legacy of inculturated Christianity after the latter's death in 1597 (Hyland 2003, 195–236); they are apocryphal works ascribed to Valera by Jesuits who shared his vision of Andean Christianity.[5] The renowned Jesuit scholar Borja de Medina has suggested that these documents represent "a fictitious composition originating in the climate of conflict between creoles and peninsulars" in the early seventeenth century, in which one side took Valera as their symbolic leader (Albó 1998, 344; Medina 1999). Likewise, R. T. Zuidema has pointed out that these texts are "very much in line with the Jesuits' reinterpretation of Inca culture for propagandistic purposes," a reinterpretation popular among certain groups of Jesuits in Peru in the seventeenth century (Mumford 2000, 45). In the Jesuit archives in Rome, Maurizio Gnerre found a letter written in the same hand as *Exsul Immeritus*, signed BV and containing explicit references to the work *Exsul Immeritus*. This letter, dated 1618, was addressed to Acquaviva's successor as Jesuit General, Muzio Vitelleschi, indicating that he at least had some familiarity with the production of these sensitive documents based on the scandal that occurred during his predecessor's administration (Gnerre 2001).

The Politics of Translation

We may never know the full story of Valera's "heresy," especially given that "heresy" itself is a highly mutable concept, whose definition depends greatly upon particular historical circumstances. What may have been "heretical" within the Society of Jesus in the late sixteenth century, when the Jesuits were beset by the efforts of the Inquisition and the Crown to limit their autonomy, would not necessarily have been "heretical" within an established mendicant order such as the Franciscans. One suspects that General Acquaviva had this in mind when he suggested that Valera simply transfer to one of

---

5. It is worth noting that the documents' claim that Valera wrote the lengthy work the *Nueva corónica y buen gobierno*, attributed to Guaman Poma, is contradicted by substantial evidence.

the mendicant orders in Peru. Certainly Valera held political views that his Jesuit superiors had explicitly forbidden to be expressed by Jesuits in Peru. The surviving excerpts from Valera's writings reveal that he questioned Spain's legal rights to the Inca Empire (Miró Quesada 1971, 255); he criticized Spanish atrocities, such as the murder of Emperor Atahuallpa (Anello Oliva 1998, 138–39); and he lauded Inca civilization and religion (see Hyland 2003, 104–21).

Yet what was the role of grammar and translation in Valera's thought? The Jesuit author stated quite clearly that Quechua—the language of the Inca Empire—was equal to Latin as a sacred tongue and was superior to Spanish or other European vernaculars. "The courtly language," he wrote, referring to Quechua, "has this noteworthy property, that it has the same value to Peruvian Indians as Latin to us" (cited in Garcilaso de la Vega 1987, 410). Learning Quechua, he claimed, conferred profound spiritual and intellectual benefits to its speakers, "turn[ing] savages into civilized and conversable men" (410). It was, he continued, the ideal language for Christian evangelization:

> [Quechua] makes the Indians keener in understanding and more tractable and ingenious in what they learn. . . . Thus the Puquinas, Collas, Urus, Yuncas, and other rude and wild tribes, who speak even their own languages ill, seem to cast off their roughness and savagery when they learn the language of Cuzco, and begin to aspire to a more civilized and courtly life, while their minds rise to higher things. Moreover, they grow better adapted to receive the doctrine of the Catholic Faith, and of course preachers who know this tongue well take pleasure in standing up to discuss higher things . . . for just as the Indians who speak this tongue are of keener and more capacious intelligence, so also the language itself has greater scope and a wider variety of elegant ornaments (409–10).

However, this elevated view of Quechua did not prevail among many of the elites within Spanish Peru and in Spain itself. The Spanish Crown, together with the Council of the Indies, which decided administrative policy for Spanish America, repeatedly called upon the Peruvian viceroys to force the Andean peoples to learn Spanish and forget their own tongues. The reason for this ruling was clear; as the

Council stated, "it is understood that [even] in the greatest and most perfect language of the Indians it is not possible to explain well . . . the Mysteries of the Faith, without great absurdities or imperfections" (Solórzano Pereyra 1995, 549; my translation). The great Spanish jurist Juan Solórzano Pereyra, who had acted as an administrator in central Peru before returning to Spain to serve on the Council, believed strongly that Andean Indians should be forced to replace their native languages with Spanish (547–54). He argued that once the native chiefs (*kurakas*) were made to learn Spanish, all of their followers would imitate them, and the process would move forward quickly. Solórzano, citing the writings of the Jesuit José de Acosta, Valera's superior in Peru, affirmed that it was not possible to explain Christian theology to the Indians in their own language. For example, Acosta had written that "if we try to find in the Indian languages any words corresponding to this one, God, as it is *Deus* in Latin and *Theos* in Greek, and *El* in Hebrew . . . it cannot be found in the language of Cuzco, nor in the Mexican tongue" (Acosta 2002, 257).[6]

Moreover, Solórzano continued, once the natives had been taught Spanish, they should be obliged to adopt Spanish clothing and other customs. As he stated, "This which has been said about obliging the Indians to [speak] our language has persuaded me that . . . they should also be obliged to [adopt] our apparel and manner of dressing and the rest of our admirable customs" (Solórzano Pereyra 1995, 554; my translation). In other words, for Solórzano, using the language of Castile also implied embracing Spanish culture.

In light of these opinions, one can appreciate the radical nature of Blas Valera and other Jesuits like him, such as Anello Oliva, who believed that Indian languages already possessed concepts appropriate for Christianity. Valera, of course, used Aymara religious terms in his translation of the catechism, a move that was not followed by the translators of the Quechua version. *An Account of the Ancient Customs* makes the case throughout the text that the Andean faith is a solid basis for Christianization, and provides many Quechua equivalences for Roman Catholic religious terms, such as *Illa* for "God" and *villca* for "priest." The Peruvian Church, on the whole, took a middle path between the royal legislation on language and the opinion of

---

6. The *Account* contradicts this statement by Acosta on the very first page, claiming that the Quechua word *Illa* "is the same as *El*, Hebrew; *Ela*, Syriac; *Theos*, Greek; *Deus*, Latin."

radicals like Valera. The policy of the Peruvian church councils by the 1580s was to allow Andeans to maintain their language and to publish religious texts in Quechua, but to keep most theological terms in Spanish.[7]

As is seen in Solórzano's writing on the subject, the issue of language policy was closely tied to that of inculturation. Jesuit opinion in Peru about inculturation had changed markedly between 1568 and 1583, when Valera was first imprisoned. The early Jesuits in Peru had embraced the use of Andean songs, dances, and customs in Catholic rituals (for example, in Huarochiri) but soon rejected the presence of Andean culture within Christian celebrations as corrupting. Yet the *Account of the Ancient Customs*, written in 1594, holds to an earlier Jesuit view of faith in the Andes, one in which the mountainsides had once been filled by hermits known as *huancaquilli* and by nuns called *acllas*, all vowed to *tito* (chastity) and *huñicuy* (obedience) and dedicated to the Supreme God, Illa Tecce, and his angels, *hayhuay panti*, the "resplendent, beautiful ones."

---

7. For an analysis of the Peruvian church's policy on language and translation, see Durston 2007; MacCormack 2007, 170–201.

3

Sources

Understanding the sources of information used by Valera in the *Account* reveals something of the heterodox nature of this work. One of the writers whom Valera criticizes most strongly, Polo de Ondegardo, was a revered font of information about the Incas in colonial Peru; Valera's criticisms of Polo go very much against the mainstream of colonial thought about Andean civilization. Many other voices included in the *Account* are from little known or forgotten pro-Indian authors, such as the Mercedarian Melchior Hernández and the Inca nobleman Don Luis Inca. The *Account* is invaluable for bringing these otherwise unknown works to the fore. Finally, unlike most other chronicles of the Andes, the *Account* relies heavily upon *khipus,* the mysterious knotted-string texts of the Incas, for knowledge of Inca civilization and religion. Valera's extensive citations from *khipus,* particularly in matters of religion, fly in the face of colonial restrictions on *khipu* use over fears of their allegedly "idolatrous" and "demonic" nature.

Polo de Ondegardo

Certainly one of the most important writers mentioned in the *Account* is Polo de Ondegardo, a Spanish lawyer, mine owner, and judge (Presta and Julien 2008). Born in Valladolid, Spain, around 1520, Polo arrived in Peru in 1544 with his uncle, Agustín de Zárate, who had been given the position of accountant in Peru. As a reward for service on behalf of the king, Polo was granted an *encomienda* of Indian labor service in Cochabamba (modern-day Bolivia). In subsequent years he served as judge, administrator, and treasurer in the silver-mining center of Potosí, where he wrote a report claiming that the natives were well treated in the mines and happy to be performing free labor service there. During the rebellion of Francisco Hernández Girón (1553–55), he fought on the side of the Spanish Crown, receiving injuries that left him permanently disfigured. Twice he served as the administrative judge (*corregidor*) in Cuzco; toward the end of his life he composed a report about the Chiriguanaes tribe to assist the viceroy in preparing a military campaign against them.

In the course of Polo's career he wrote numerous influential reports that were widely copied and quoted. Many of his original writings have been lost, existing only in summaries or in extracts. For example, one of his most famous works, the *Tratado y averiguación sobre los errores y supersticiones de los Indios* (Treatise and inquiry into the errors and superstitions of the Indians), published by the Lima Council of Bishops in 1583, is an extract from a much longer work that no longer exists.

Throughout the first half of the *Account*, Valera harshly criticizes Polo's writings about the Indians. Arguing that Polo's ignorance of the Quechua language made him unable to understand his native informants, Valera accuses Polo of inventing most of his "facts." Specifically, Valera refutes the following claims made by Polo: (1) that the Incas sacrificed hundreds of humans at a time; (2) that the Incas sacrificed the sacred virgins (*acllas*); and (3) that the Incas shared many customs with the Spaniards' hated enemies, the Moors, including their method of animal sacrifice, their manner of eating, and their ritual bathing (*opacuna*). Valera expresses particular frustration with the influence that Polo had on other scholars of the Indies; as he writes, "But because [Polo] was a judge and learned, and was the first to write about Peruvian antiquities, other learned writers have been allowed to take so much from him that, without questioning anything that he wrote, they transfer his lies to their books."

One of the writers most heavily influenced by Polo was, in fact, Valera's Jesuit superior, José de Acosta. As Sabine MacCormack has written, "Acosta's guide in all matters of Andean religion was Polo de Ondegardo, whom he often quoted verbatim" (MacCormack 1991, 269). Valera clearly could not directly criticize Acosta, to whom he owed obedience. However, in each instance where Valera refutes Polo, he is also refuting a claim made by Acosta in the latter's recently published work, the *Natural and Moral History of the Indies*. Using Polo as his source, Acosta states that: (1) the Incas sacrificed hundreds of human beings (Acosta 2002, 291–93); (2) the Incas ritually

sacrificed consecrated virgins (282–83); and (3) the Incas practiced
Moorish rituals, including their style of animal sacrifice (289), their
style of eating (290), and their ritual lavations (305–6). In the *Natu-
ral and Moral History,* Acosta used these characterizations of the
Incas to develop a hierarchy of non-Christian nations in which the
Incas were below the Aztecs, the Chinese, and the classical civilizations of ancient Greece and Rome (MacCormack 1991, 249–80).
By criticizing Polo in the *Account,* Valera is disputing the basis of
Acosta's conclusions about the nature of Inca religion and civilization. For Valera, who possessed a profound, "insider's" view of native
Peruvian culture, the Inca Empire was not only on par with the
greatest civilizations of classical antiquity, but even surpassed them
in many important respects.[1] His critique of Polo, whose work was
used by Acosta to justify a relatively negative view of the Incas, helps
to lay the foundation for Valera's more positive appreciation of Inca
civilization.

Melchior Hernández, O. de M.

By far the most frequently cited author in the *Account* is the Mercedarian friar Melchior Hernández. Like Valera, Hernández was born
of an Indian mother and a Spanish father and was noted for his great
linguistic abilities. He apparently came from the region of modern-
day La Paz, Bolivia, where he was a Mercedarian friar by May of
1572. Later that year he was in Cuzco, where he ministered to the
captured Inca emperor Tupac Amaru (Barriga 1954,182–83). By 1579
he was assigned to the Mercedarian house in Potosí; there he came
to the attention of the Peruvian Inquisition for the attempted rape
of three Indian girls (AHN 1579–80). After his acquittal on grounds
of insufficient evidence, he was sent to Ayacucho, Quito, and finally
Panama (Molina 1973–74, 2:173, 349, 373). He is known to have
written a catechism in Quechua (Murúa 1987, 485; Molina 1973–74,
2:173), now lost, as well as an ethnographic account of the indigenous
people of Panama (Hernández 1996).

1. Valera's discussion of religion was highly influenced by the writings of the
ancient Roman author Marcus Terentius Varro, as quoted by Saint Augustine of Hippo.
For an analysis of how Varro's categories of "mythical theology," "civil theology," and
"natural theology" are used by Valera in the *Account,* see Hyland 2003, 150–60.

Valera was in Potosi at the same time as Hernández, and it is quite likely that the two missionaries, both of mixed Indian and Spanish heritage and sharing an interest in Inca antiquities, knew each other there. According to the *Account*, Hernández composed two additional texts, *La interpretación de las oraciones antiguas* (The interpretation of ancient prayers) and *Anotaciones* (Annotations).

Valera cites the first text for its discussion of the Inca gods Pirua and Viracocha and for its interpretation of the Inca funeral prayers, which revealed that the Incas did not worship the dead. Valera refers more frequently to the *Annotations*, citing its definitions of the numerous Quechua words to demonstrate his interpretations of gods, sacrifice, and confession in the Andes.[2] Unfortunately, both of these texts have been lost and are known only through their citations in the *Account*.

Other Writers

One of the most intriguing aspects of Valera's writings is his references to numerous works, like those of Melchior Hernández, that are now lost and known only through those references. One that seems to have been of particular importance to Valera was Francisco Falcón's *Apologia pro Indis* (Defense of the Indians), which, according to Valera, Falcón composed as a refutation of Polo de Ondegardo's descriptions of the Incas. Valera cites the *Defense* five times on matters of native Peruvian deities, sacrificial rites, liturgical prayers, and sacred temples. Falcon's chapter on native leaders ("De Praetoribus"), Valera states, argued that "there has never been among the gentiles any kings more benign and clement than the Incas." This work has disappeared without any other trace, although Falcón's other work defending Inca civilization, his account given to the Lima Council of Bishops in 1567, still exists (Falcón 1918). Valera apparently knew Falcón in Lima, where the latter testified that Valera was a moral person who greatly assisted the Indians (Hyland 2004).

Another lost source employed by Valera is *Anotaciones de la lengua* (Annotations on the language), a discussion of the Quechua

---

2. Valera cites Hernández's definitions of the following words: *Pirua, Viracocha, Tocapu, Punchao, Opacuna, Huaminca, Harpai, Huaspai, Huahua,* and *Nacai*.

language by Juan de Montoya, a fellow Jesuit. Montoya was one of the most learned men in Peru, having received a doctorate in theology from the Jesuit college in Rome, where he taught before leaving for Peru (*Monumenta peruana 1966–86*, 2:117). He was the Jesuit representative at the Second Lima Council of Bishops, where he would have become familiar with Falcon's representation to the council. Possessing a gift for languages, Montoya was fluent in both Quechua and Aymara. He is known to have written a history of the different regions of Peru that has been lost. Montoya lived in Juli while Valera was there, and it may well have been in Juli that Valera had the opportunity to see Montoya's text on the Quechua language.

Francisco de Chaves, a kinsman of Valera's father, Luis, wrote a "copious" account of the conquest that he gave to Luis Valera, according to the Jesuit chronicler. Valera writes that this text, now lost, was passed on to the conquistador Diego de Olivares, whom Blas knew in Trujillo. Chaves's text, Valera states, was cited by Juan de Oliva in his *Annales* (Annals) and by Diego Alvarez in his work entitled *De titulis regni piruani* (Concerning the title to the kingdom of Peru).

Little is known about Diego Alvarez other than that he was a Spanish attorney and a leading citizen and *encomendero* in Huanuco; he was also a close friend of Francisco Falcón (Lohmann Villena 1970, 143). According to Valera, Alvarez was informed about native customs by the Indians of his *encomienda*. Other lost works referred to in the *Account* include Friar Marcos Jofre's *Itinerario* (Itinerary); Friar Mateo de los Angeles's *De ritibus indorum* (Concerning the rites of the Indians), Juan de Oliva's *Annals;* Falconio Aragonés's *De libertate indorum servanda* (On preserving the liberty of the Indians); and works by two priests, Cristobal de Molina and Juan de Montalvo, both excellent Quechua scholars, according to Valera.

Most valuably, Valera had access to a written text, referred to as the *Advertencias* (Notices), by an Inca nobleman, Don Luis Inca, who was probably a member of Valera's confraternity in Cuzco that met for weekly "spiritual" discussions. Valera cites Don Luis's account in support of his statement that the ancient Peruvians worshiped only the sun, moon, and stars represented as idols, rather than the idols themselves. Valera also refers to this work, which was written in Don Luis's own hand, when discussing Inca ritual sacrifices. Like the other texts mentioned above, it has disappeared since the time Valera was able to consult it.

Years ago, the scholar Lohmann Villena proposed that there was a core of pro-Indian writers in Peru in the 1560s and 1570s whose work is virtually unknown (Lohmann Villena 1970, 134). The investigations of the colonial writers cited by Valera, from Hernández to Falcón to Luis Inca, form a substratum of writings about Andean people from the sixteenth century that are unknown to modern researchers. As long as these texts remain lost, we can know something of their contents only through the writings of Blas Valera.

Khipus as Sources

Account of the Ancient Customs of the Natives of Peru cites *khipus* as sources more than any other colonial Andean chronicle (Brokaw 2010, 147–49). *Khipus* (also written *quipus* or *quipos*) were knotted and colored cords that were used to record information throughout the Inca Empire. In general, a *khipu* consisted of a primary cord from which hung colored woolen or cotton pendant threads. The position and number of the knots tied onto the pendant threads provided numerical information based on the decimal system. The kind of knot used indicated the number, while its position on the string indicated whether it was a unit of one, ten, one hundred, or higher (for the structure of the *khipu*, see Urton 2003, 1–8). Most *khipus* appear to have been used for recording numerical information relevant to Inca accounting. A special, tax-exempt class of individuals, known as *khipukamayus*, were skilled in the use of *khipus* and were charged with keeping records of labor tax service, births and deaths, the contents of state storehouses, the distribution of state goods, military service, and so on.

While it is clear that *khipus* encoded numerical information, Spanish accounts tell us that they also recorded histories, biographies, and other forms of narrative. In his examination of some 450 *khipus* in museum collections around the world, Gary Urton has found that roughly two-thirds have their knots tied and organized in a manner to indicate numerical values (2003, 53–55). The remaining one-third have their knots tied in ways that violate the principles of decimal registration. These "anomalous" *khipus* apparently were constructed to retain information for the production of narrative accounts. Although it is unclear how *khipus* may have recorded narratives,

Urton has theorized that they encoded information through binary sequences that stored units of information. In the multiple steps of the *khipu*-making process, including choosing the fiber, spinning it, plying it into strings, dyeing the strings, and attaching them to the primary cord, binary, either/or choices had to be made. Urton has argued that these choices were the components of a binary coding system that enabled *khipukamayus* to represent data narratives such as histories and biographies.

Throughout the first half of the *Account*, *khipus* are referred to repeatedly as sources alongside written texts, such as Melchior Hernández's *Interpretation of Ancient Prayers* and *Annotations*. The names of two different authors or creators (*camayus*) of *khipus* are provided in the text: Francisco Yutu Inga and Juan Huallpa Inga. According to the marginal notes in the manuscript, the *khipus* of these two men indicated that the ancient Peruvians worshipped only the sun, moon, and stars; that the Peruvians never worshipped the devil under the name *Supay*; and that human beings were never offered as sacrifices in the Inca Empire. It is quite likely that both Inca noblemen were members of the Nombre de Jesús confraternity, where they engaged in weekly conversations about Christianity and Andean religion with Valera. Juan Huallpa was a particularly important member of the Inca nobility; according to a report made in Cuzco in 1571, he had been the keeper of the king's wardrobe during the time of Emperor Huayna Capac (Montesinos 1882, 211).

Other *khipus* referred to in the *Account* are anonymous, indicated primarily by their geographical point of origin. *Khipus* from the following locations are cited as sources of information: Quito, Cuzco, Cajamarca ("Cassamarca"), Huamachuco, Chincha, Tarma ("Tarama"), Condesuyu (the western quarter of the empire), and Collasuyu (the southern quarter of the empire). Additionally, the author refers to the *khipus* of three shrines—Pachacamac (a major oracle on the Pacific coast), Sacsahuaman (Cuzco's fortress, which also served a religious function), and Pacari Tampu (the place of origin for the Incas; see Urton 1990). Because *khipu* records were kept at every level of the Inca administrative hierarchy, as well as at shrines and any other important location of human activity, *khipus* from all of the places listed would have indeed existed during the Inca period. The author of the *Account* claims that these *khipus* provided information about a variety of topics, including the benefits for which the people prayed to the sun; the meaning of the term *pirua* (granary); the death of Pirua Pacaric Manco; how offerings were given to the gods; lists of temples and shrines; lists of items sacrificed to the gods; lists of gods worshipped; and, finally, "the very long disputation" of Amaro Toco, philosopher and wise man, in which "he proved that no one born of a man and a woman could be a god." This final item can be found, according to the text, only on the *khipus* of Cuzco and Sacsahuman; no written sources are mentioned in connection with Amaro Toco.

While there is no evidence in the *Account* of the *khipu*-based biographical narratives found in other chroniclers (Brokaw 2003; see also Julien 2000), the types of information claimed for the *khipus* in this text are in agreement with what we know about *khipus* from other sources. Several Spanish chroniclers assert that Inca officials kept detailed ritual, calendrical, and astronomical *khipus*, as well as genealogical/historical ones (Urton 2003, 53). Therefore, the types of *khipu* data cited in the *Account*, such as items offered to the gods, lists of shrines and temples, or the biography of the philosopher Amaro Toco, could reasonably have been expected to have been on the *khipus* mentioned in the text. The anonymity of these *khipus* is striking, and suggests that the author was reflecting upon many years of traveling to the places mentioned, where he spoke with either the *khipukamayus* themselves or with native Andeans who had derived their information from *khipu*-based recitations.

The early sixteenth-century Spanish colonial administration in Peru was dependent upon *khipu* records, for census, tribute and production data, and *khipu*-based accounts find their way into numerous Spanish administrative reports. However, by the 1580s a shift began in how *khipus* were viewed by the colonial elites within the Andes. As Carmen Beatriz Loza has argued, by 1583 the use of *khipus* was under attack by the Lima Episcopal Council because of the medium's suspected ties to Andean paganism (Loza 1998). The decrees of the 1583 Lima Council ordered all *khipus* with links to Andean ritual or calendrical data to be destroyed. From the late 1580s onwards, Loza continues, colonial *khipukamayus* were forced to work semiclandestinely for fear of being discovered in a practice that colonial authorities linked to idolatry. While we now know that *khipus* continued to be used locally in the Andes throughout the seventeenth century (Salomon 2004, 118–20), their secular use was officially denigrated and appears to have gone underground.

The one area in which Andeans were officially permitted to continue *khipu* use throughout the colonial period was related to missionary activities. The Jesuits particularly encouraged Andean Christians to use *khipus* for confessing their sins (Durston 2007, 286; Brokaw 2010, 234–42), allowing Indians to knot their sins on the *khipu* for confession to a priest. Jesuits also allowed natives to use *khipus* to memorize Christian prayers such as the Our Father and the Hail Mary.[3] It is noteworthy that both types of evangelical *khipus* advocated by the Jesuits—confessional *khipus* and prayer *khipus*—were for private, individual memorization. That is, they did not have to be "read" by anyone beyond the individual who created the *khipus*. In fact, one of the confessional *khipus* described in the Jesuit Annual Letter from Cuzco in 1602 was a highly idiosyncratic affair, including stones, bones, and feathers and requiring four days to recite (Cabredo 1986, 214). A seventeenth-century Jesuit chronicler of the Incas claimed that *khipus* served only as mnemonic devices and were inferior to European writing: "Even among the *quipoca-mayos* [*khipukamayus*] themselves, one was unable to understand the registers and recording devices of the others" (Cobo 1983, 254). For Acosta, the Incas' lack of a valid writing system was an important reason for the inferiority of Andean civilization when compared to ancient Mexico, China, Greece, and Rome (Acosta 2002, 334–44; Mignolo 2002, 510).[4]

One can appreciate, therefore, Valera's boldness in the *Account* when he presents *khipus* as texts capable of conveying sacred thought in all its complexity. In contrast to the Jesuits' narrow use of *khipus* for individual confession and prayer memorization, he

3. The Jesuits' limited use of *khipus* in evangelization contrasts strongly with the practices of the Mercedarians. According to the missionary instructions of the Mercedarian Diego de Porres, written between 1572 and 1579 when Porres was vicar of Santa Cruz de la Sierra, *khipus* were (1) to be used to encode all of the decrees of the Lima Bishops' Council and given to the head of the community; (2) to be used to encode the list of the thirty-four obligations of the *varayocs* (community leaders) and given to them; (3) to be used to encode the Christian calendar indicating religious holidays and placed in the church for all to see; (4) to be used to create an inventory of the goods of each Indian when he or she dies and given to the heirs and the priest; and (5) to be used to encode the Our Father, the Hail Mary, the Apostle's Creed, and the Hail Holy Queen along with the Ten Commandments and given to the faithful (Porres 1954).

4. Acosta writes, "Before the Spaniards came the Indians of Peru had no kind of writing at all, either by letters or characters or ciphers or pictures, like those of China or Mexico" (2002, 342).

proudly cites *khipus* as important and unique sources of knowledge, referring specifically to their religious and ritual content in a positive light. Implicit in Valera's reliance on *khipus* for sacred information is the notion that *khipus* form a fully functioning writing system, as capable of communication as any European or classical writing system. The same *khipus* that had been condemned by the 1583 Lima Council as examples of pagan idolatry are here portrayed as sacred purveyors of an ancient religious faith in harmony with the Christianity that was to come.

Notes Concerning This Translation

This translation is based on a photocopy of the original manuscript in the National Library in Madrid, no. 3177. The emphasis of this translation has been on readability for students, while retaining accuracy. Foreign (i.e., non-Spanish) words have been kept in the text in order to demonstrate the author's use of language. In the case of Latin words and phrases, the original Latin has been maintained, followed by an English translation in brackets. Likewise, Quechua and Aymara words have been kept in the text. When the meaning of the word is not immediately explained by the surrounding text, the English meaning of the word has been supplied in brackets the first time the word is used. The spelling of the Quechua and Aymara words follows that of the original manuscript. A glossary of indigenous terms follows the text.

Notes in two late sixteenth-century hands are written into the margins of the original manuscript. In this translation, these notes have been presented as footnotes to the text. The editor's comments appear as footnotes in brackets.

Three short portions of the *Account* have been left out of this translation because they are not relevant to the themes of religion that dominate the text: (1) civil customs of the ancient Peruvians; (2) Inca laws; and (3) the natural conditions of the Peruvians. Interested students may consult these in the Spanish edition prepared by Henrique Urbano and Ana Sánchez (1992).

Blas Valera, *An Account of the Ancient Customs of the Natives of Peru*

Concerning Religion

The Peruvians believed and said that the world, the heavens and the earth, and the sun and the moon were created by another being who was greater than they were: this being they called *Illa Tecce*, which means Eternal Light.[1] Modern peoples added another title, which is *Viracocha*, meaning the great god of Pirua; that is, he whom Pirua, the first inhabitant of these provinces, worshipped, and from whom all of the land and empire took the name of Pirua, which the Spaniards corruptly call Peru or Piru.

The devil forced them to think that this immense and true God had imparted his divinity and power to various creatures so that each one would act according to the office or virtue that it had. And these gods were the companions and advisors to the great God, and mainly were in the heavens, as are the sun, the moon, the stars and the planets. Thus, the people of Peru passed a great many years without idols, without statues, without images, because they worshipped only the luminaries of the sky and the stars.[2]

They said that the sun was the child of the great *Illa Tecce*, and that the sun's corporeal light was part of the divinity that *Illa Tecce* had given to him, so that the sun would rule and govern the days, the seasons, the years and summers, and the kings and kingdoms and lords and other things.[3] They said that the moon was the sister and wife of the sun, and that *Illa Tecce* had given part of his divinity to her and

1. Illa is the same as El, Hebrew; Ela, Syriac; Theos, Greek; Deus, Latin. Tecce is the same as principium rerum sine principio ["first thing without beginning"]. [Valera's note; notes added by the editor are enclosed in brackets.]

2. Authors: Polo in the Inquiry; Juan de Oliva in his Annals, the beginning; Friar Melchior Hernández in his Annotations, the word Tocapu; the quipos of Iutu Ynga and those of Huallpa Inga, and the common tradition.

3. Authors: the same, and Friar Melchior in the word Punchao and Licenciado Falcon in his apologia pro indis [Defense of the Indians] num. 85, and various quipos.

made her the lady of the sea and of the winds and of the queens and princesses and of childbirth for women, and queen of heaven.[4] The aurora,[5] they said, was the goddess of maidens and of princesses and the maker of the flowers of the field, and the lady of the dawn and of twilight and of the colored clouds. She threw the dew upon the earth when she shook her hair, and thus she was called *Chasca*. They called Jupiter *Pirua*,[6] saying, first, that the great *Illa Tecce* had ordered this planet to be the guardian[7] and lord of the empire and provinces of Piru, and of its republic and of its lands. Because of this all of the provinces sacrificed their harvests to him, along with everything that seemed most noteworthy and outstanding by nature, such as in the ears or grains of corn or in other harvests and the fruits of trees.[8] To this god they entrusted their granaries, their treasures, and their storerooms; because of this they called the most remarkable ears of corn or those that were first harvested, and the repositories that they kept in their homes to guard their treasures and clothes, dishes, and weapons, *Pirua*.[9] Second, they said that when the great Pirua Pacaric Manco Inca,[10] the first populator of these lands, died, he was carried into heaven to the house and place of this god named Pirua, and there he was lodged and feted by this god.[11]

4. They called her Coya, Queen.

5. Chasca.

6. All of the quipos and memorials of Cusco and of the rest of the provinces, and the common usage that everyone sees today in the language.

7. Pirua.

8. [Examples of "noteworthy" agricultural products include doubled ears of corn, individual grains of an unusual color, or fruits and tubers of an irregular shape.]

9. [Montesinos cites the following description of the god Pirua: "they gave this name Pirua to the Creator of things with great mystery. . . . [T]hey held as a sure tradition that this name was very ancient and therefore it was given to the Creator of all things, and also because, just as in the storehouses were stored and kept the seeds and all things necessary for human sustenance, so all things were in the Creator without lacking anything" (in Hyland 2007, 92–93).]

10. [The name Pirua Pacaric Manco Inca for the first pre-Inca Peruvian king is found only in one other text, the anonymous Quito manuscript preserved by the seventeenth-century priest Fernando de Montesinos. In general, the *Account of the Ancient Customs* shares the unique and heterodox chronology of Peruvian kings found in the Quito manuscript (Hyland 2007). Montesinos cites the following description of the god Pirua: "they gave this name Pirua to the Creator of things with great mystery. . . . [T]hey held as a sure tradition that this name was very ancient and therefore it was given to the Creator of all things, and also because, just as in the storehouses were stored and kept the seeds and all things necessary for human sustenance, so all things were in the Creator without lacking anything" (in Hyland 2007, 92–93).]

11. The ancient quipos of Pacari tampu and Friar Melchior Hernández in The Interpretation of the Ancient Prayers and in his Annotations, the words Pirua and Viracocha.

They said that Mars[12] was in charge of the things of war and of soldiers. Mercury[13] was in charge of merchants and travelers and messengers. Saturn[14] was in charge of plagues and massacres and starvation and of the lightning and thunder; and they said that this god went about with a cudgel and with his bows and arrows to wound and punish men for their wickedness.[15]

To other stars, such as the signs of the zodiac, they assigned various duties, some to care for and guard and nourish sheep [llamas and alpacas], others lions [pumas], others serpents, others plants, and thus the rest of all things.

Later,[16] some nations were given to say that in[17] each one of these gods or stars existed the ideas or models of those things they had under their care or specialty; and thus they said that such and such a star had the shape of a lamb because its job was to guard and preserve the sheep; such and such a star the shape of a lion, such and such a star the shape of a serpent. And it was agreed that here in the land they would make statues or images of these ideas or things, according to the duties that each one had. And in this way began the idols of stone, wood, gold and silver, which they said represented the gods that were in the heavens; although later they said that those statues were the same ideas.

They also said that the great *Illa Tecce Viracocha* had invisible servants[18] because the Invisible must be served by invisible beings. They said that these servants were created out of nothing by the hand of the great God Illa Tecce, and that of these, some remained in his service, and these they called *Huaminca*, soldiers and loyal and constant servants, or *Hayhuay panti*, resplendent beautiful ones; others were false and became enemy traitors, and these they called *çupay*, which properly means evil adversary. In this way they worshipped the *Huamincas* as gods and even made statues and idols of them. But they

12. Aucayoc.

13. Catuilla.

14. Haucha.

15. [These attributes of Jupiter, Mars, Mercury, and Saturn are derived from classical antiquity and not from Andean beliefs about the stars.]

16. Authors: Polo in his Account, sub medium, and the others cited above, and Don Luys Inga in his Account.

17. The great God Illa Tecce had certain ideas of all things present and to come, and that for the good government of the world he distributed these ideas to each one.

18. Huaminca, good angel, miles coelestis [heavenly soldier].

never worshipped the devil under this name, *çupay*,[19] or that which they understood to be *çupay*.[20] And thus the devil invented other various ways in which these gentiles could worship him. Idols were called *Villcas* and not *Huacas*.

Sacrifices

Sacrifices usually were of livestock that they had domesticated, called *Huacayhua, llama, urcu, huanaco*, and *paco*, which are what the Spaniards call "rams or sheep of the land."[21] They also used to sacrifice dogs, either black ones or white ones. They could kill lions [pumas] and snakes to serve the god of war, sacrificing the heart or head. *Anta* [tapir] is an animal similar to a wild bull without horns, and this they also used to sacrifice to the god of animals.

They used to sacrifice grains, roots, medicinal herbs, especially the two they call *coca* [*Erythroxylum coca*] and *sayri—sayri* is that which by another name they call tobacco—bird feathers, shells from the sea, or the pieces made from these shells called *mollo* [*Spondylus*], woolen clothing, gold, silver, metal, and fragrant wood. This fragrant wood was not offered as a sacrifice, but served as the firewood to burn all of the other things; it was also a superstition that the firewood had to be sweet-smelling, just as it was that the chosen heads of livestock had to be of such and such an age and such and such a color, and not in any other manner.

They also used to sacrifice some little animals that they call *cuy* [guinea pig] and various birds and other fowl for different necessities. In their method of killing the beasts or birds, they kept the same order maintained by the Greek and Roman gentiles, as the poets Homer and Virgil and others recount. The Peruvians did not, as Polo invents through conjecture, keep any ceremony of the Moors, who

19. [By the late sixteenth century it was common in Peru for the word *supay* (*çupay*) to be translated by the Christian concept of "demon." Its older Andean meaning is the shade or light, volatile part of a living being (Duviols 1978).]

20. This is against Friar Domingo de Santo Thomas. Authors: Juan de Oliva ubi supra [cited above]. Friar Agustín [sic; the author's name is Jerónimo] Roman, augustinian, in the Indian Republic, book , chap.[blank in the original], Francisco Yutu, Juan Huallpa, Ingas, and Don Sebastián, Lord of Guarochiri, Diego Roca Inga, Friar Melchior Hernández, word Huaminca.

21. Polo with the rest.

never traveled to these lands, nor could teach to the Peruvians their veneration towards Mecca nor any rite whatsoever from their Koran. It was likewise a deception to say that the natives of Peru used to stuff themselves and have a boisterous second meal, in the manner of Moors, when the stars appeared, because the opposite is what used to happen. And by star, it is not the evening star, but the morning star, the brilliant one called *Chasca*, which is meant. They used to fast from the day before until the morning star became invisible because of the presence of the sun. And then they ate their ordinary food, not dog flesh as Polo wants to indicate, but deer and birds and lambs. And there was never among them any ceremony or ritual of eating a noisy second meal, unless all of the things of the Roman gentiles we wish to apply to the Moors, and call them by their names, as Polo himself does.[22]

There Was No Sacrifice of Men or of Children Among the Peruvians[23]

But the worst error (or, if it must be said) false testimony that Polo stated about the Peruvians was that they used to sacrifice adult men

22. Licenciado Falcón in the Apologia pro Indis that he presented to President Lope Garcia de Castro against Polo and León and other writings by some malicious soldiers. Friar Melchior Hernández, expressly, in the words Arpai and Nacai. Juan de Oliva, as eyewitness, and he was one of the first conquistadors; Friar Marcos Jofre, Franciscan, who was twice provincial in Peru, in his Itinerario [Itinerary] titled, De modo sacrificandi indorum [Concerning the Indian manner of sacrifice]. The quipos of Cuzco, of Cassamarca, of Quito, of Humanchuco, and the common opinion; and particularly Don Luis Inga, in the Notices that he wrote by hand in his language.

23. Authors are all of those already mentioned, but in particular Francisco de Chaves, of Xerez, who was a great friend of Tito Atauchi, brother of King Atahuallpa, who not only was informed about a thousand things, but who saw with his own eyes that which is said here, and wrote an extensive account that he left in the care of his friend and kinsman, Luis Valera, and the latter gave it to Diego de Olivares, from whom Juan de Oliva—who was also an eyewitness—and Licenciado Alvarez, citizen of Huanuco, took it for his book, De titulis regni piruani [Concerning the title to the kingdom of Peru], in the chapter, De sacrificiis [Concerning sacrifice]. Apart from Chaves's book, he was informed by the Indians on his encomienda. Friar Marcos Jofre is also against Polo in his Itinerario, and there he cites Francisco de Chaves and Juan de Oliva and Friar Matheo de los Angeles, Franciscan, who wrote De ritibus indorum [Concerning Indian rituals], and died as a saint in Cassamarca. Item: Licenciado Falcón, in the Apologia pro indis, in the chapter, De praetoribus [Concerning the chief magistrates] says that there has never been among the gentiles any kings more benign and clement than the Ingas. Friar Melchior Hernández, of the Order of Our Lady of Mercy, in his Annotations, the

and women and children for various needs.[24] Polo conducted his investigation in Cuzco, being a judge in the year 1554, when the language was barely even known and there were no interpreters, nor was there any place to learn the ancient things from their roots.[25] Thus, he could not keep from writing many things contrary to what used to happen and to how the Indians understood them; because it is certain and verified that most of what he wrote was by means of conjecture, in the way of commentaries, because to one word that an Indian spoke, he added a hundred as interpreting and explaining that word; and of this there is already such clear evidence in many instances that one can barely read in his papers anything that is not full of his conjectures. But because he was a judge and learned, and was the first to write about Peruvian antiquities, other learned writers have been allowed to take so much from him that, without questioning anything that he wrote, they transfer his lies to their books. And he who made the compendium of Polo was allowed to take these lies, by the same fraud, saying that in the coronation of the kings, two hundred children were sacrificed, as it is referred to in the little book of rites of the Indians (*De ritibus indorum*, in 2, p c. 9, no. 3).

The reason it is proven to be a lie, first, is because there was a very ancient law of the kingdom and of the kings that prohibited sacrificing humans or human blood, as being a very cruel thing and pertaining only to the Caribbean Indians. And this law was kept so carefully that it is not known that at any time anyone has dared to break it—I am not saying the lords—but the Inga himself. It is a tradition that this is because the great Pirua, first populator of the land, ordered this.[26]

---

words Arpai, Aspai, and Huahua. Don Luis and Don Francisco Yutu, Juan Huallpa, Diego Roca, Don Sebastián Nina Villca, Lord of Guarochirí, Don Juan Collque, Lord of the Quillacas, in the quipos and memorials. All of the quipos of Pachacamac, Chincha, Contisuyo, Collasuyo and of Cuzco agree, and from them these reasons have been taken.

24. Note that Polo reversed everything; that which pertained to the Andes he applied to the Ingas, and the reverse, because he did not then have any understanding of the antiquities of Peru other than what they told him in confusion, because he arrived already very late to the kingdom.

25. Polo did his investigation when the marquis of Cañete, the senior, had just arrived to the kingdom. At this time all the Indian historians and elderly men had fled to the forests because of the uprising of Francisco Hernández Girón that occurred in the year [1553].

26. The quipus of Cusco, of Cassamarca, of Tarama, of Quito and of other provinces.

The second reason is because each time when the Ingas conquered some provinces of the Andes of people who ate human flesh, the first thing that the Ingas ordered, on pain of death, was that they not eat, much less sacrifice, men or children. And if such people had a law allowing human sacrifice, later it was revoked on orders that they not follow it. Thus, it is clear that if the Inga permitted the sacrifice of humans in Peru, he would have allowed this in the Andes, where we see that all of the jungle Indians who were conquered by Topa Inca Yupanqui[27] in Quixos, Motirones, Moyopampas, Ruparupa, Villcabamba, and others, do not have this vice; and when the Spaniards came they found in these places, among these people, those who had eaten human flesh before being conquered.

The third reason is because the Ingas valued being always merciful, and on the day of the king's coronation they ordered all of the prisoners—even those who deserved death because of their crimes—to be released. How does it follow that they would allow so many children to die, when they granted and conceded life to so many ruffians? This would be a great cruelty and against their own laws, even though executing ruffians was just.

The fourth reason is because their laws established a greater penalty for those who killed or sacrificed a child than an adult man. Moreover, it is false to say that the Peruvians broke their laws so easily; they kept them as carefully as they kept other laws of lesser importance and of a smaller penalty, as even Polo admits and praises greatly.

The fifth reason is because even in times of triumphs, when the victors entered Cusco and brought with them the captured captains and soldiers, none of the latter died under the law as a sacrifice. On the contrary, there was a law ordering that the prisoners die as traitors and enemies, just as the Romans had also for their triumphs which they carried out in the midst of their celebrations;[28] only, for the Ingas, in place of the human prisoners who were to die, so many heads of livestock were given to be sacrificed, and these were called *runa* [men], that is, llamas that die for men. And Polo did not understand the truth of this history and interpretation. Later, *a fortiori* [with yet stronger reason], it remained that at the time of the Inga

27. [According to the traditions of Inca historians in Cuzco, Topa Inca Yupanqui was the tenth Inca emperor and the father of Emperor Huayna Capac.]

28. Father Montoya, of the Society of Jesus, in his Annotations on the Language.

kings' coronation it was the greatest celebration and greatest mercy
to make all human bloodshed cease, which in effect did cease. To
those who say that in the Inga Huayna Capa's[29] coronation two hundred children died and one thousand adults were buried, I concede
that two hundred *huahuas* and one thousand *yuyac*—or, as others
say, *runa*—were sacrificed. But these *huahuas* did not mean children, sons and daughters of men, but baby llamas, which they also
called children in that language. And in the same way, *yuyac* means
animals already grown to adulthood that are sacrificed in the place of
humans.[30]

Temples and Sacred Places

They had two types of temples, some natural and others artificial.[31]
The natural ones were the heavens, the elements, the sea, the land,
the mountains, the jagged valleys, the copious rivers, the fountains
or springs, the ponds or deep lakes, the caves, the gashes in the living
rock, the mountain summits. The ancient Peruvians held all of these
things in reverence, not because it was understood that there existed
some divinity or virtue from heaven in them, nor that they were
living things. Rather, it was because they believed that the great *Illa
Tecce* had created and placed there that specific thing and indicated,
by its particular and singular aspects, that it was beyond what other
sites of its type commonly had. Thus, it would serve as a sacred place
and as a sanctuary where he and the other gods were worshipped.
This can be seen in the prayers that they recited when they knelt or
prostrated or stood in such a site. They did not speak with the mountain or spring or river or cave, but with the great *Illa Tecce Viracocha,*
whom they said was in the sky or invisibly in that place. And this
form of prayer was very common among the Peruvians. And in their
language, these natural sites were called by different names, such
as the mountain peaks, *apachitas,* the caves, *huaca,* the mountains,
orcos, the springs, *pucyu,* the skies, *hahua pacha.* And they did not
worship in all of the mountains and hills, all of the springs and rivers,

29. [In the traditional king lists of Inca historians in Cuzco, Huayna Capac was
the eleventh Inca emperor; he died around 1527.]
30. The dictionary of the Quechua language printed in Lima, the word Huahua.
31. The quipus already mentioned.

but only in those where there was some singularity worthy of particular consideration, holding them as sacred spots. And the modern peoples added that when the minor gods came to the land, sent by the great God, they rested in such places and left them consecrated. And without doubt the devil appeared to some of the gentiles in similar places in the image of some god that they imagined, such as *Pirua*, Jupiter, or *Huacha*, Saturn, etc. so that he would be worshipped in such sites when they passed by them; he would favor them and hear them, although he was not present. The Peruvians used this type of natural temple for a long time without constructing any buildings. And when there were many, they built a stone altar, called *osno*, in such sites for their sacrifices.

As time went on, they began to build low temples in high places, and little by little the temples came to the towns and cities, where they were constructed with a sumptuousness shown in the shrines and ruins that remain and that we all have seen.

Their temples were always spacious, with one aisle and a type of main chapel. On the wall they made stone altars where they placed the golden or silver idol; the temple and the altar had the decorations appropriate for the idol. The temple of the great *Illa Tecce Viracocha* that is in Cusco and is now the cathedral church, dedicated to Our Lady, had nothing more than an altar in the same spot where the main altar is now. And on that altar there was a stone idol of marble, the height of a man, whose hair, face, clothing and shoes were in the same style as the apostle Saint Bartholomew. A Spanish inspector and administrator of the district of Los Canchis (where the gentiles had hidden the statue) later smashed this idol into pieces. The altar was of the same worked marble, and the temple was adorned with tapestries of very fine wool. Sweet-smelling things and grains were offered on the altar and in the atrium, which had wide steps, they burned the sacrifices.

The Temple of the Sun, which is now the Church of Saint Dominic, had another altar, and a golden idol painted like the sun with its rays in a niche in the wall; in honor of this idol the altar and the walls were covered with sheets of gold, and even the external sealant of the building was of molten gold. Here there was a fire they used to call eternal, in the manner of the Romans, because it had to be lit perpetually by night and by day. Virgins, who were like the vestals of Rome, cared for this fire.

The temple of the planet called *Pirua* was everywhere adorned with flowers, harvested grains, lights, and with a certain type of lamp. The idol made in memory of the god *Pirua* always held fresh bouquets or fistfuls of grain in his hand. The temple of the sign of Scorpion was low, with a metal idol made in the shape of a serpent or a dragon with a scorpion in the mouth. Almost no one entered this temple unless they were sorcerers. This temple had large atriums for sacrifices; with its atriums it was called *Amaro cancha* [snake enclosure], where the Society of Jesus now has its school. In the same place where the snake idol used to be in ancient times, there is now the main altar containing the Tabernacle of the Most Holy Sacrament.[32]

In Cusco there was a temple, like the Pantheon of Rome, where all the idols from all the nations and peoples subject to the Inga were placed. Each idol stood in its altar with its insignia, but with a chain around the foot to signify the subjugation and vassalage of its people.

There were many other temples in Cusco, and each province or nation throughout the kingdom had its decorated temples and its ministers. And the temples were called *huaca*.

Another type of temple they had were the graves of the dead built in the countryside. By coincidence, just as today a Christian will choose for himself and his relatives some sepulcher, and even decorate it according to his wealth, thus also the Peruvians did in ancient times, choosing and building sepulchers in the countryside or in the barren places. The sepulcher of the king and the great lords was like a house for the living, with its reception room, bed chamber, and dressing room, with all of the other places necessary for the larder, kitchen, patios, hallways, porters, etc. They removed the intestines from the dead king or lord and embalmed his entire body with balsam brought from Tolu and with other preservatives, in such a way that a corpse embalmed like this lasted more than four hundred or five hundred years. The funeral was solemn, with its own type of hymns. They used a style of liturgy where they brought out the deceased seated, dressed very well, and after having done the obsequies and laments in the atriums, they put the corpse in the main chamber or in the dwelling that had been prepared for this.

---

32. [The *Amarucancha* compound was built as the royal palace of Emperor Huascar during his short rule (ca. 1528–32). It included a large, round ceremonial tower for sacred rituals, the *Sunturwasi* (excellent house), which was torn down to build the Jesuit church.]

They seated him there and closed up the door and windows. And in the antechamber they placed all his treasures and dishes and clothing, and offered much food, like bread and wine made from his kernels of maize. Later a law or public announcement was sent forth that any of his manservants or maids or friends or confederates who wished to go to serve that lord in the other life could volunteer to do so. This was desirable because, for one thing, the great *Illa Tecce Viracocha*, creator of the sun and moon and stars and heavens and earth, and lord of all the other gods, would reward them very well. Second, the particular god of the deceased's family and nation would be favorable to them in the other life and would give them all things in abundance. Third, the children and heirs of those who thus wished to go to the other life to serve the deceased would be given here a very great abundance of lands and necessary goods from those that belonged to their fathers, and from others out of charity. And he or she who did not wish to go to the other life offered to assist the deceased with all the necessary offerings here in this life. Those who wished to obey that law and public announcement did so in one of three ways: some killed themselves voluntarily by their own hand or by the hand of another whom they chose and in the manner of death that they wanted. And thus there were ropes, knives, wild beasts, steep cliffs, drinks of poison that would end life, and other types of death. And he or she who was to die went with great solemnity and accompaniment. The most common way to kill oneself was to take poison, or to let out one's blood with a flint; ropes to hang oneself were almost never used, nor steep cliffs; I don't know that wild beasts were used other than two or three times outside of Cusco. After they died, they were placed, embalmed, in the antechamber if they were men, and in the treasury if they were women. The succeeding king or lord would grant mercy to their heirs, freeing them from all obligations and tribute.

The second manner, since this death was so voluntary, was that even after having offered oneself before the magistrates, one could commute it into another service, like a sacrifice of livestock performed next to the grave. And in front of some magistrates, after giving sufficient reasons and causes for the commutation of one's death, it was publicly received. And he would then offer for himself so many heads of livestock and clothing and other things, and so many llamas for his wife, and so many llamas for his children. Not only did they call the livestock that was to die for men *runa,* men, *huarmi,* women, *huahua,* children, but they also gave to the animals the proper names of those who had offered their lives, calling the ram *Quispi,* and the ewe *Chimpu,* and the lamb *Pasña.* The sacrifice was performed very solemnly, and once finished, a great feast was held because they had satisfied death and escaped with their lives.

This type of commutation was so common among the Peruvians that it happened that most of the time no one died at the death of princes and lords, except for livestock in people's place. And with the death of Huayna Capa, emperor (who died in Quito), not even ten people died, but livestock who reached the number of a thousand, because there were many who offered themselves and made this commutation, and the livestock remained indicated in the histories with the title and name of men, as we already noted about Huayna Capa above. And thus this is seen to be the truth, first, because in all of the sepulchers and *huacas* that the Spaniards ransacked through-out the realm to take out treasure, they did not find a single Indian, but only clothes and treasures in the chambers where the lords were interred. And if they found some bones and skulls of the dead, they were not from Indians who were killed because of that superstition, but who had died from sickness or plague, since they were outside the *huacas* and did not have any of the signs that were ordered to be placed on such human sacrifices. Second, because that commutation of death to sacrifices of animals and offerings was taken among them to as more than sufficient, and thus it came about that the kings con-sidered this better than if there were dead, which would cause horror and more lamentations and sorrow.

The third manner of offering oneself to the law was to vow always to go offer food and drink to the deceased, scattering it in the sepul-cher at certain times, and to serve as a minister. And because of this there were many people who went to the sepulchers, not only to those of kings and lords, but of private individuals too.

Many times, these sepulchers or *huacas* were easily seen, except for the chambers where the deceased and his treasures were because these had the doors and windows blocked off. But the atriums, por-tals, rooms, and other areas were open so that people could enter to pray to the gods for the deceased and to watch over them in shifts and vigils; the vigilance that they had in honoring and guarding and preserving their dead was great. And the main reason for this was that the Ingas and their *amautas* (thus they called their wise men), principally, believed that souls would return to their bodies at a certain time and be revivified, adding that this would not happen unless the corpses were maintained incorrupt without missing anything, at least of their bones, since the flesh wasted away. Because of this they took excessive care in interring their deceased embalmed, or covered with a certain confection that, in the absence of balsam, preserved the flesh so that it would be preserved. And Polo touches upon this issue of resurrection when he says that the Peruvians believe that their dead kings and lords must return to this life, although in another place he denies their belief in resurrection.

After some cruel wars and various floods occurred, they began enclosing the sepulchers, not only the doors and windows, but throwing earth on top, creating tombs and mounds like hills over them. Nonetheless, the locations of some remained in people's memory, but, when it was learned throughout the kingdom that the Spaniards had entered the land with an armed hand, robbing, killing, destroying temples and shrines, sacking towns, and that their whole hearts were devoted to silver and gold, the Peruvians agreed to cover and hide all of the sepulchers. And they threw into the sea or lakes the treasures that they could not hide.

It can be seen in the words of the prayers recited by the Peruvian gentiles that they did not worship the dead, even if they were the bodies of kings, nor did they worship anything that was in those sepulchers, called *huacas*.[33] Nor did they believe that there existed in the *huacas* or in the dead any divinity or power from heaven. Rather, they mainly begged and pleaded with the great *Illa Tecce* to watch very carefully over the deceased, and not allow his body to decay or become lost here on the earth, nor allow his soul to walk about, roaming and wandering. But they asked *Illa Tecce* to take in the soul and put it in a place of contentment, and to receive those offerings or sacrifices that were given for the deceased, and order that they be given to the dead person so that he or she could enjoy that which was sacrificed. And later they asked other gods to intercede for the one praying and for the deceased, so that the great *Illa Tecce Viracocha* would grant everything that had been requested.

33. Authors: Polo, in The Account of the Orations of the Inca. Friar Melchior Hernández, in The Interpretation and Explanation of them. Licenciate Falcón, in the Apologia pro Indis.

Polo says that there were Ingas who wished to be worshipped like gods, and who ordered the people to treat them this way; however, it is clear that was merely his conjecture, because in the histories and memorials of the ancient and modern Indians this idea cannot be found, but rather its opposite.[34] This is revealed in a very long disputation that Amaro Toco, *amauta*, had in Cusco in the time of the Ingas.[35] In this he proved that no one born of a man and a woman could be a god, because if one man could, then all other men could also, and thus there would be a confusion of gods, which was not useful for anyone. And this disputation greatly pleased the Inga who lived then, and because of it he made a law that no one could worship an earthly mortal man, neither in life nor in death, under the penalty of death, nor could anyone try to do so, under the same penalty. And if some king, deceived by pride, said that yes, he was a god, or ordered himself or his statue to be worshipped thus, then for the same reason he was unworthy of his realm and it could be taken from him.

This law preceded by many years Huayna Capac, who Polo says particularly wished to be a god. And the truth is that Huayna Capac was the most scrupulous about keeping the laws of his forefathers, and not only did not try to make himself worshipped, but even confirmed and reestablished that law. This was repeated later in the time of his son, the king Atahuallpa,[36] in a gathering that he organized in Cassamarca, in a type of parliament.[37]

Certainly it is true that some Ingas created statues, calling them *huaoque*, brothers, and giving them sacrifices, priests, and rents. However, this was not a statue of himself, in his name and representing his person. Rather, it was of a god held particularly by the family, or nation, or house from which he came, or of some special god that he thought had been favorable and pious toward him (and whom they want to call *hauque*) in such and such a thing. And this can be seen to be so because, after the death of such an Inga, when his statue was carried in procession because of some family necessity, they did

34. Thus says Falcón in his Apologia pro Indis, and Friar Melchior Hernández.

35. The quipos of Cusco and of Sacsahuaman.

36. [After Emperor Huayna Capac's death, two of his sons, Atahuallpa (centered in Quito) and Huascar (centered in Cuzco), fought a civil war for control of the empire. Atahuallpa's generals had captured the capitol, Cuzco, and defeated Huascar's forces when Spanish conquistadors arrived and took Atahuallpa prisoner in 1532.]

37. The quipos of Quito, where the said Huayna Capac died; Francisco de Chaves, in his Account.

bracelets and armbands of gold and precious stones, and his footwear was of fine wool. Once the sacrifice or incense burning was finished, he removed these vestments and remained in his ordinary habit. He could not be married nor have any loose woman with him; he maintained his continence all his life, inasmuch as the election to his office was lifelong. He had a substantial income in all the provinces of the kingdom, and shared it among the poor, especially the blind, crippled, widowed, orphaned, and he did not take more than necessary for his sustenance and for the decorum of his office. This *Vilahoma* selected the vicars who were in each province, enlarging or limiting their jurisdiction; he confirmed the election of judges and the president, as we said above, in matters concerning their religion. He had to be an *amauta*, wise and of illustrious lineage, who was everywhere free of tribute obligations. And if it were understood that he suffered from some deficiency in this, the election was nullified. However, if he were a great *amauta* and a very worthy man, the question of his lineage was ignored, on condition that he have at least some illustrious blood from his father's side.

At certain times, he used to provide inspectors to investigate all of the ministers of the idols and temples and sanctuaries, without exempting anyone. Other inspectors, distinct from the former, he used to send to investigate the monasteries of people who lived as religious, men as well as women, of whom there were a great number in Cusco and throughout the entire realm. He created other inspectors, distinct from the rest, for the people in order to examine and punish the excesses or faults and crimes that they had committed against their false religion and against their gods. Another, more terrible effort that he undertook, so that these inspections would be more effective, was that he secretly sent some person or persons whom he trusted to observe how the inspectors performed their office, if they received bribes, if they robbed the people or committed other evils. And finding any of this, he was very severe in the punishment that he gave them, perpetually depriving them of their office and condemning them to the mines or to serve in the temples, sweeping and carrying firewood.

One thing that must be greatly admired, because such a thing is written of no other ancient or modern gentiles, is that this *Vilahoma* elected and chose confessors, so that in Cusco, as in all of the other provinces and towns, they would secretly confess everyone, men and

not speak to the dead Inga, but to *Illa Tecce* primarily, and later to that particular god as an intercessor, and they prayed to one and to the other for the deceased Inga.

Primary Ministers

In the great Pirua, there were three different types of ministers for the idols, temples, and sacrifices.

The first, who were in charge of instruction in the things of their false religion, were the masters of the ceremonies and rites that they used to practice. These priests taught the people the number of their gods, and idols or statues, and declared the laws and rules about their religion that had been made by either the kings, or the republic, or the high priest, who was like the supreme pontiff. They promulgated newly made laws, oversaw the interpretation of the laws, and determined the answer to any questions that occurred, as much among the other priests as among the people.

From among these were elected certain judges who knew and punished all of the crimes and evil acts, excesses, and careless actions that were committed against their false religion; among these judges there was one who was like a president and who governed them. From among these was elected the great *Vilahoma*,[38] who was like the supreme pontiff, who had jurisdiction over the kings in ancient times. However, after Topa Inca Yupanqui, they gave the *Vilahoma* and the rest of the ministers a great demotion, not only in authority and power, but also in lineage and income, for reasons that we will explain below.

The great *Vilahoma* was like the supreme arbiter and judge in matters of religion and of the temples, who was recognized and reverenced by the kings and lords and all of the people and the priests. His life was that of a monk, very abstemious: he never ate meat, but only herbs and roots, accompanied by a type of cornbread; his house was in the countryside, and very rarely in populated places; his speech was infrequent. His dress was ordinary, plain, of wool, but very modest, falling to the ankles like a cassock, and over this a very large mantle,

38. [*Vilahoma* is a Spanish colonial creolization of the Quechua phrase *Willaq umu*. Valera may have chosen to use *Vilahoma* instead of a more accurate rendering (such as *Huillac umu*) to show the phrase as a general term equivalent to "pope."]

either gray or black or purple. He did not drink wine, but always water. Living in the countryside was for the purpose of contemplating and meditating more freely on the stars, which he regarded as gods, and on the matters of his religion. For the principal festivals he would go to serve in the temples of the great *Illa Tecce*, or the sun or *Pirua*. And to light incense, or to make a sacrifice or offering, he dressed in the following manner: a great tiara on his head, which was in the style of a hood or close-fitting cap, that was like this:

They used to call this the *Vila chucu*. On top of this he placed the rest of the framework, which was a large golden medallion made like the sun, and above this a great diadem, and below the chin a half moon of gold, and around the edges, long feathers from the large parrots they call *guacamayas*, in this fashion:

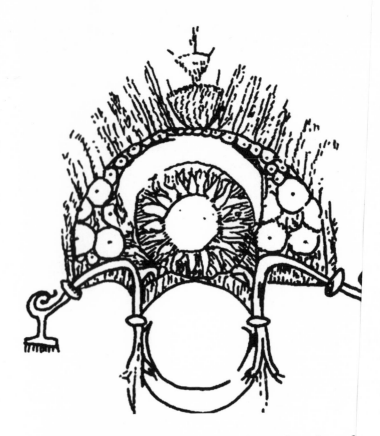

All of this was covered with little golden discs and jewels; and used to call the entire headdress *Huampar chucu*.[39] Then this followed by a garment like a cassock or tunic without sleeves, to the floor, loose, without a belt, and over this a *huapil*, that i sleeveless surplice of white wool, falling to the knee, with frir borders of red wool, and all of the *huapil* covered with a scatt of small golden discs and some jewels. In place of sleeves, the

39. [A Jesuit priest writing in the seventeenth century described the rit gear and clothes of the local Andean priests thus: "They have been allowed t their half-moons of silver, called *chacrahinca*; the objects called *huamas*; an diadems or round plates which they call *tincurpa*, some of which are copper, silver, and not a few of gold; the shirts overlaid with silver and the *huaracas* upon their heads with silver buttons and plumes of various colors" (Arriaga

not speak to the dead Inga, but to *Illa Tecce* primarily, and later to that particular god as an intercessor, and they prayed to one and to the other for the deceased Inga.

Primary Ministers

In the great Pirua, there were three different types of ministers for the idols, temples, and sacrifices.

The first, who were in charge of instruction in the things of their false religion, were the masters of the ceremonies and rites that they used to practice. These priests taught the people the number of their gods, and idols or statues, and declared the laws and rules about their religion that had been made by either the kings, or the republic, or the high priest, who was like the supreme pontiff. They promulgated newly made laws, oversaw the interpretation of the laws, and determined the answer to any questions that occurred, as much among the other priests as among the people.

From among these were elected certain judges who knew and punished all of the crimes and evil acts, excesses, and careless actions that were committed against their false religion; among these judges there was one who was like a president and who governed them. From among these was elected the great *Vilahoma*,[38] who was like the supreme pontiff, who had jurisdiction over the kings in ancient times. However, after Topa Inca Yupanqui, they gave the *Vilahoma* and the rest of the ministers a great demotion, not only in authority and power, but also in lineage and income, for reasons that we will explain below.

The great *Vilahoma* was like the supreme arbiter and judge in matters of religion and of the temples, who was recognized and reverenced by the kings and lords and all of the people and the priests. His life was that of a monk, very abstemious: he never ate meat, but only herbs and roots, accompanied by a type of cornbread; his house was in the countryside, and very rarely in populated places; his speech was infrequent. His dress was ordinary, plain, of wool, but very modest, falling to the ankles like a cassock, and over this a very large mantle,

38. [*Vilahoma* is a Spanish colonial creolization of the Quechua phrase *Willaq umu*. Valera may have chosen to use *Vilahoma* instead of a more accurate rendering (such as *Huillac umu*) to show the phrase as a general term equivalent to "pope."]

either gray or black or purple. He did not drink wine, but always water. Living in the countryside was for the purpose of contemplating and meditating more freely on the stars, which he regarded as gods, and on the matters of his religion. For the principal festivals he would go to serve in the temples of the great *Illa Tecce*, or the sun or *Pirua*. And to light incense, or to make a sacrifice or offering, he dressed in the following manner: a great tiara on his head, which was in the style of a hood or close-fitting cap, that was like this:

They used to call this the *Vila chucu*. On top of this he placed the rest of the framework, which was a large golden medallion made like the sun, and above this a great diadem, and below the chin a half moon of gold, and around the edges, long feathers from the large parrots they call *guacamayas*, in this fashion:

All of this was covered with little golden discs and jewels; and they
used to call the entire headdress *Huampar chucu*.[39] Then this was
followed by a garment like a cassock or tunic without sleeves, falling
to the floor, loose, without a belt, and over this a *huapil*, that is, a
sleeveless surplice of white wool, falling to the knee, with fringes or
borders of red wool, and all of the *huapil* covered with a scattering
of small golden discs and some jewels. In place of sleeves, there were

39. [A Jesuit priest writing in the seventeenth century described the ritual headgear and clothes of the local Andean priests thus: "They have been allowed to keep
their half-moons of silver, called *chacrahinca;* the objects called *huamas;* and others like
diadems or round plates which they call *tincurpa,* some of which are copper, some of
silver, and not a few of gold; the shirts overlaid with silver and the *huaracas* they wear
upon their heads with silver buttons and plumes of various colors" (Arriaga 1968, 69).]

bracelets and armbands of gold and precious stones, and his footwear was of fine wool. Once the sacrifice or incense burning was finished, he removed these vestments and remained in his ordinary habit. He could not be married nor have any loose woman with him; he maintained his continence all his life, inasmuch as the election to his office was lifelong. He had a substantial income in all the provinces of the kingdom, and shared it among the poor, especially the blind, crippled, widowed, orphaned, and he did not take more than necessary for his sustenance and for the decorum of his office. This *Vilahoma* selected the vicars who were in each province, enlarging or limiting their jurisdiction; he confirmed the election of judges and the president, as we said above, in matters concerning their religion. He had to be an *amauta*, wise and of illustrious lineage, who was everywhere free of tribute obligations. And if it were understood that he suffered from some deficiency in this, the election was nullified. However, if he were a great *amauta* and a very worthy man, the question of his lineage was ignored, on condition that he have at least some illustrious blood from his father's side.

At certain times, he used to provide inspectors to investigate all of the ministers of the idols and temples and sanctuaries, without exempting anyone. Other inspectors, distinct from the former, he used to send to investigate the monasteries of people who lived as religious, men as well as women, of whom there were a great number in Cusco and throughout the entire realm. He created other inspectors, distinct from the rest, for the people in order to examine and punish the excesses or faults and crimes that they had committed against their false religion and against their gods. Another, more terrible effort that he undertook, so that these inspections would be more effective, was that he secretly sent some person or persons whom he trusted to observe how the inspectors performed their office, if they received bribes, if they robbed the people or committed other evils. And finding any of this, he was very severe in the punishment that he gave them, perpetually depriving them of their office and condemning them to the mines or to serve in the temples, sweeping and carrying firewood.

One thing that must be greatly admired, because such a thing is written of no other ancient or modern gentiles, is that this *Vilahoma* elected and chose confessors, so that in Cusco, as in all of the other provinces and towns, they would secretly confess everyone, men and women, hearing their sins and giving penances for them. He ordered that they keep secret everything they had heard, on the pain of death. He enlarged or limited the power of the confessors, and reserved for himself or for his vicars certain cases. The confessors of the virgins who were enclosed in the temple had to be eunuchs or men who had vowed perpetual chastity, and usually they were old, elderly men.

No new god could be received or worshipped without a decree from the *Vilahoma*. He used to choose the kingdom's historians so that they could fix in their memorials all of the deeds of the *Vilahoma* and of the priests, of the kings and of the lords. And he picked someone to examine the histories done in this way, so that they would be certain and true. New temples could not be constructed without his permission, and without the income that corresponded to their ornamentation. When he died, all of the people gathered together and lamented him for an entire day. Embalming him, they buried him with much pomp on some high mountain. And later, after the burial, the priests and primary ministers of all different kinds, and those who attended for the king, and the procurators from the town where he died and from the kingdom, and the *amautas*—not all, but those chosen by him who had this task—gathered in the temple and there picked who would be the next *Vilahoma*. The election did not lack ambition and conflict, although at times it was done without noise, very peacefully. Later, as word of the elect left, they played all their trumpets and horns and other instruments that served for the sacrifices, and in that same day they crowned him in the temple, putting the *Huampar Chucu*, or miter, and his vestments on him and performing various sacrifices. And later the kings and queens and princes and caciques and lords and all the other ministers pledged him their obedience; they came to kiss his right hand, and carried him to his house. And he vowed again, for a second time, to live in perpetual chastity and continence, and as for the rest, it happened as has already been said.

From that first type of minister came those who were like prelates in the towns and provinces, and the vicars and inspectors. The prelates were like bishops, and they were few; in the entire kingdom there were not even ten. In Collao, there was one; in Collasuyos, another; in Contisuyos, another; in Chincha, another; in Huaylas, another; in greater Cassamarca, another; in Ayahuaca, another; in Quito, another; and for the Muchicas, another, whose seat was in the great *huaca* that is in Trujillo, that the natives call Chimo. So that altogether there were nine, and all of the provinces were divided up among them, each one already having knowledge of his territory. Some say that in Canas and Canchis, next to Cusco, there was another *Villca* (thus these men like prelates were called), and if this is true, there were ten; and all recognized the great *Vilahoma*. And even if they had been elected and put into office by the preceding *Vilahoma*, they still asked for confirmation and new authority from the newly elected *Vilahoma*. These *Villca* chose the rest of the minor ministers for sacrifices. At the time of their election and the confirmation of their office, these *Villca* vowed, at the hands of the great *Vilahoma*, continence and perpetual chastity until death (because their office lasted for their whole lives). They had already made this vow earlier when they had become ministers and priests of the idols, but now it was ratified again with more solemnity, and at the same time they promised obedience to the present or future *Vilahoma*.

From this it can be seen that all of the ministers and priests of this first class, the higher ones as well as the lower ones, were not married, nor could they marry according to their laws. If they were caught in adultery or rape, they would experience the law's rigor without mercy, which was a very severe and violent corporal death. And if they were caught having compromised themselves with women who were neither married nor maidens, they were deprived of office for a certain length of time for the first offense. If caught for a third time, they were deprived of office for life. They lived in a cloister, as we will explain later when we discuss monks and nuns. The priests that came after the *Villcas* were called *Yanavillcas*.

Diviners

The second class of ministers were those whose task was to foresee coming events, or to see things in the present, but very far away from the location in which they were; these individuals commonly were called *Huatuc,* that is, diviners. Among these were the ones who read omens and who received the oracle in the temple. These *Huatuc* were celibate and could not marry at any time, at least not during their term of office. They went about dressed in brown; they could not eat meat except for certain days of the year during solemn festivals; they ate herbs and roots and grains of corn; they were almost always to be found in the atriums of the temples.

The divinations that they performed were through observing the flight of birds, or the intestines of sacrificial animals, or tokens that they threw, or the contemplation of the stars and the constellations, or the answers given by the oracles. They had a pact with the devil, who responded to them, not through all of the idols, but only through a few most noteworthy, so that these would be more revered. Such was the oracle of *Mullipampa* in Quito, and of *Pacasmayo* in the valleys of Trujillo, and of *Rimac* in Lima, and that of *Pachacama*, and that of *Titicaca*, or, as others call it, *Inticaca*, in the province of Collao. When it was time to hear the oracle, the aforesaid minister was possessed by a diabolical furor that they call *utirayay*, and afterwards he would declare to the people what the oracle had told him. These particular ministers were properly called *Huatuc;* but those who read omens from the flight of birds, or from the intestines of animals that they or others killed, were called *Hamurpa*. Their role was not to kill or cut open the animals, because other ministers did this. The *Hamurpa* did not do anything else besides examine the intestines and the blood, along with their positions, and thus prognosticate, declaring the evil or good omens. Those who were to be the *ichuris*, that is, the confessors who heard the sins of everyone in the towns, were elected from among these ministers. For this they had to be very learned in the things of their gods and their religion, similar to those of the first type of priests, because otherwise they could not perform this office. And for this there were examiners, that is, four wise *amautas* with one *Hatun villca*, who was like a prelate or a bishop. They examined the candidates first about the number of gods, and the rites and the ceremonies, and the laws that the *Vilahomas* and the Inga kings had established, and in their declaration, and about the different sins and penances that were given for each one. In this way, when they were found to be knowledgeable about all of these things, they were approved as confessors, reserving certain sins for the great *Vilahoma.*

The manner of confessing was next to a river, and the confessor gathered by hand a big fistful of hay or grass and held it in his right hand. In his left he gripped a small, hard stone attached to a cord or inserted into a hole made in a handheld stick. Seated, he called the penitent, who came trembling, and prostrated himself fully before the confessor. The confessor commanded him to get up from the

ground and be seated; he exhorted him to tell the truth and not
to hide anything because he, as a diviner, knew more or less what
the penitent had done. With this, the penitent did not dare to hide
anything. The confession had to be heard in secret, and the *ichuri* or
confessor carefully kept the natural secret. If it were said about him
that he had broadcast the sins of someone who had been his penitent
and that he had heard in confession, he would die for that without
pardon. The sins that they confessed were these:

worshipping another god apart from those that were received
by the whole republic; speaking ill of some god; execrating or
cursing oneself or another person (because they never used
positive oaths, such as "I swear to God," "as God lives," or "I
vow to God" and other similar ones, nor did they know what
such curses were); cursing oneself with a lie before a judge,
such as "may the earth swallow me," "may the lightning strike
me," etc. (because this was the manner of swearing that they
had in their lawsuits before the judges); not celebrating their
festivals; not attending sacrifices when they were obliged to do
so; cheating a sacrifice of the offerings or animals that they had
the obligation to bring; dishonoring by word and by deed their
father and mother, their grandparents and aunts and uncles; not
obeying them; not helping them with their needs; not obeying the commands of the *Vilahoma*, nor of the *Hatun villca*,
or dishonoring them and the other major and minor ministers;
not obeying the king; attempting a rebellion against the king
or speaking ill of or murmuring against him (that concerning
a rebellion was a case reserved for the *Vilahoma*; worshipping
another god apart from those they had, or speaking ill of a god
were reserved cases also); killing a child or an adult outside of
a just war; a judge killing someone out of vengeance; being the
cause of an abortion, especially if the woman had conceived at
least three months before; raping a virgin,[40] or sacrilege and
rape combined against some vestal virgin (and this was also a
case reserved for the *Vilahoma*); committing adultery with a
married woman, or a married man with any woman; forcing
any woman, even if she were a whore; committing fornication

40. And this was a case reserved for the Hatun Villca.

with single women, widows and sluts; committing a sin against nature with another man or with animals; stealing the value of a *fanegada* of corn or of potatoes, which are a kind of truffle; robbing on the highways; plundering during wartime without permission of one's captain; spreading malicious gossip; lying to cause harm; having been lazy sometime during the year; and not having attended to one's duties or one's turn of work.

These are the sins that they used to confess, although some simpletons did not discuss their evil desires, either because they did not know them or because the priests did not suggest it to everyone. Those who were well instructed definitely used to declare their interior sins, like hatred and abhorrence, the intention to carry out a revolt, or to show some desire to sin with a virgin or a married or public woman, and even more if the desires were to sin with the queen or a princess or some noblewoman of the kingdom—whom they used to call *ñusta*—or with some vestal virgin. They also declared their desire and intention to steal. And thus, when some say that Peruvians did not declare interior sins, they are speaking of the simpletons or of children who did not know, but the Indians who were taught certainly did declare them.

Once the penitent finished speaking, if the confessor saw that he had uncovered all of his heart, the confessor did not attempt to extract more, but exhorted him to mend his ways and to worship their gods, and to obey the great *Vilahoma* or the *Inga*; and whether he was rich or poor, the penitent was given the same penance according to the sins he had confessed. And concerning what Polo says that the poor were given very harsh penances because they were poor, it has to be understood that they did not do this from greed, for, as Polo himself admits in many places, they were very detached from that; nor was it from snobbery toward the lowly either, because they would go to help the poor with equal care as the rich. The reason was because the rich and powerful could make satisfaction for their evil acts within a populated area, making restitution through giving to the temples, to the blind, to the lame, to the mute, to the crippled, and to orphans, in the amount they were ordered to as their penance. Sending them to the desert would be too obvious, because they would be gone for a long absence and they would be missed in the town, and later it would be realized that they had committed the gravest sins because they have been given such a penance. Nonetheless, if some wealthy or powerful person wished to go to the wilderness for fasting and solitude, he could certainly do so and did so. Regarding the poor and the commoners, since they were so innumerable, no notice at all was taken if they were sent to the desert as a penance and were there a long time. For one thing, it was very common, and for another, it was not noteworthy, and finally, the poor person could not make satisfaction within a populated area because he did not have an estate. The solitude of the wilderness or wasteland was not so great because in it there were already many Indians who voluntarily performed there the harshest penances, eating roots and drinking water; and many did this their whole life as a type of hermit. And thus it was not wearisome for the penitents to go to perform their penance because communication with each other was unavoidable.

Once the confessor gave the penance and some soft blows on the back with a small stone, the two spat on the handful of hay or grass, although the penitent spat first, and the confessor recited certain prayers, speaking with their gods and cursing sin. Then they threw the handful of grass into the river and asked the gods to carry it to the abyss and hide it there forever.

If the confessor saw that the penitent had not uncovered his heart fully, or if he suspected this, the confessor then performed there the sacrifice of a *cuy*, which is like a little rabbit or a very large rat, or of another animal or whatever vermin. Opening the animal and performing his incantations and witchcraft, he said that he had divined that the latter had hidden sins from him, and, giving it to him with the stone, the confessor made the penitent reveal all that he had hidden; and in all the rest it was as it has been said.

The *Inga* and the *Vilahoma* ordinarily did not confess with anyone. Instead, the Inga went to the river or to some creek with his fistful of newly plucked hay or grass, and there he spoke with the sun and asked him to forgive his sins—promising that he would amend his faults, and that the river or creek would carry them away to the abyss. And having said this, he spat on the handful and threw it into the water, and thus ended his confession. And it is untrue that he then performed a lavation, called *opacuna*,[41] and even less true

41. Author: Friar Melchior Hernandez, in his Annotations, the word Opacuna, says that the lavation was not used in the rite of confession, although it was used in other sacrifices that served as expiation.

that these lavations could be compared to those of the Moors, called *guadoi*. Because as Polo presented his conjectures about each thing, it seemed to him that in this matter there was also a lavation, and that it would be very similar to those of the Arabs, and what he imagined he put down as history. In any case, neither the Inga nor his subjects used to employ lavations in their confessions, but rather used to imitate the *Vilahoma* in this.

The *Vilahoma* used to confess to the great *Illa Tecce* in the temple, holding in his hand a fistful of hay, of flowers, and of some sweet-smelling herbs. Spitting into his hands, he sacrificed the plants and threw them into the fire, and asked that the smoke carry away his sins. He would take the ashes and carry them to the river or stream, and having said his prayers he would throw them into the water for them to sink. He neither washed nor performed *opacuna*, and returned to his house. It is still known that sometimes the Ingas and even the *Vilahomas* confessed to certain principal ministers who were maintained as personal confessors and who had an income and much authority because of it.

It is said that the *ichuris* confessors were principally *huatuc*, diviners, and they had to be men and not women, at least in Cusco and among the Chinchaisuyos, and even among the Collas. Later, with the humbling of the ministers and the ensuing disorder, it was planned that women would confess women, and men, men; but this was not kept except among some Collas.

Sacrifices

Humu

The third class of ministers consisted of those whom we call *Humu*, sorcerer, and *Nacac*, butcher or flayer of animals for sacrifice. These ministers were like servants and assistants to those of the first and second rank. Their principal duty was to adorn the temples, cleaning them and providing everything necessary for the sacrifices: firewood, flowers, branches, animals, birds, clothing, coca, fat, seashells, bread, wine, grains, fruits, ovens, roasters, plates, cups of gold or of silver. They killed the animal, flayed it, opened it, and observed it to see what it portended, and they prognosticated by the entrails and the liver; and, according to this, they washed the meat this many or that many times, they roasted it or boiled it, or did to it according to what was determined.[42] If they sacrificed flesh with blood, they said *Harpay;* if flesh without blood, *Aspay;* if oblations, like bread and grains, *Cocuy.*

At the time of the sacrifice, the singers sang many songs; they played trumpets, reed pipes, and horns made of large seashells, and bugles. When it was necessary to have their processions, called *Huacaylla* or *Tomariy,* they left accompanied by the rest of the ministers, *Yana Villcas* as well as *Huatus,* and those of the third type carried the litter on which the idol had been placed. These and the other ministers maintained themselves by the meat of the sacrifices and other offerings. These *Humus* or lay officers, if they were among those who touched the sacrifices, could not be married while they held their office; and if they married after leaving or quitting their office, they could not return to being sacrificial ministers. The rest, who served to guard the temples, cleaning them and carrying what was necessary, were married, and their wives washed and swept together and spun for the cloth that was to be woven for the temple. The ministers who watched over the sanctuaries and caves, who were like hermits, and those who kept the annual calendar, who lived in the heights to observe the shadows of the sun and the stars, were all married. All of these ministers, the major ones as well as the minor ones, except for those to whom the sacrifices and the offering fell, had a designated income of land and bolts of cloth.

All were exempt from taxes and tribute and royal jurisdiction; and if the great *Vilahoma* or some *Hatun Villca* fell into the business of a crime of *lesae majestatis* [high treason], he was deprived of office and estate and was thrown to the mines, which at that time was a most grave punishment, like the galleys; although if the case were such and so atrocious, their lives were taken by pure torture or they were handed over to the king's ministers.

The major ministers always attained their office by means of election and proofs of sufficiency. Those of the second and third type attained their office in one of three ways: by means of heredity, or by means of election, or by having been born with some singular and rare sign not found among most men, like having six fingers on a

42. [Prognostications based on animal entrails (especially of guinea pigs) are still very common in the Andes today.]

hand, or arms longer than ordinary, or having been born at the same time that a lightning bolt struck near the birthplace, or having been born feet first, or other signs. Nonetheless, the people and the king eventually struck down that of heredity.

In ancient times, all of these ministers were given great authority and respect by the Peruvians, as much because they were rich and powerful as because they were noble and well connected. During the time of Viracocha Inga,[43] however, many of these ministers were the main reason that the nation rose up and rebelled, particularly Anta Huaylla[44] with the Chinchas [Chankas], which resulted in great wars and almost the loss of the kingdom. Because of this, Tito Yupanqui,[45] son and heir of the king, rose to the challenge and defeated his enemies and arrested a great quantity of priests of the idols and brought them to Cusco. Triumphing over them, he deprived them of their offices forever. And after he came to be the absolute king, he created a new type of priest and minister, ordering that they were always to be from the commoners and poor people, and that in the case of treachery and rebellions they were subject to the penalty demanded by law, which was to suffer a cruel death. Thus he made a law changing the nature of the ministers, and their way of living, and sacrifices, such that they call him Pachacutic, which means World Reshaper, and he is the ninth of that name.[46] After, Topa Inga Yupanqui, his son, renewed this law, and even allowed women to serve by assisting in the sacrifices also, and for female confessors to hear confessions from women. From this time the women of Collasuyo began to perform this office and to observe the entrails of the small animals that they opened, and to perform other sorceries; because, before these two kings, neither married women, spinsters, nor widows held these offices, except for the vestal virgins, of which we will speak later.

For his part, the great *Vilahoma* who lived then also suffered the lash of the law. He lost much of his land and income during the time

---

43. [In the traditional, Cuzco-based chronology of Inca kings, Viracocha Inga was the eighth emperor.]

44. [Anco Ayllu, also known as Uscovilca, was the leader of the Chanka nation during the war between the Chankas and the Incas.]

45. [More commonly known as Inca Yupanqui, this ruler was famed for defeating the Chankas when the latter attempted to invade Cuzco.]

46. [Traditional Inca histories list only one emperor named Pachacutic. Only this text and the northern indigenous history preserved by Montesinos mention nine Peruvian emperors named Pachacutic (Hyland 2007).]

of all the wars because of all the looting the soldiers did; and the same was the case for the *Hatun Villcas* and the *Yana Villcas*.

Regarding these ministers' obedience toward their superiors, the ancient ones as well as the moderns, there is nothing to discuss or emphasize, because one reads that no other gentiles were as subject and obedient to those who ruled and governed them as the Peruvians. And thus, among many religious today this proverb, "the obedience of an Indian," is used to signify perfect and swift obedience. They had their decurions, whom they immediately obeyed, and these their leaders of fifty and of one hundred, and these latter their *penta* [leader of five hundred (abbrev.)—*Latin from Greek*] and *chiliarches* [leader of one thousand—*Latin from Greek*], the first one of whom was for five hundred, and the latter for a thousand, a superior called the lord of a thousand. Their exactitude in obedience was to be admired, and laziness was not allowed. The ministers who were married went to their houses on the days that they did not perform their duties. Those who were not married and had promised lifelong chastity always were in the temples and slept in the neighborhood next to the temple where they served, without mixing with other people.

Indian Monks and Hermits

The excessive zeal in searching for gold and silver shown by the Spaniards who entered Peru was part of why neither in the beginning nor in the coming years were many ancient things about the Peruvians' false religion learned. This ignorance was greatly aided by the civil wars that the Spaniards had among themselves for more than thirty years, instigated by their self-interest and greed. And if they learned anything about the religion, it was not because they wanted to learn, but because in searching for treasures, burials, and graves where there was gold and silver, and having news of some, they asked who and how the treasures were put there, along with all of the rest that thereby could be learned in order to obtain more treasure, if it existed. And this was the main reason why Polo discovered the graves of the kings and great lords of Cuzco, because he understood then that those remote recesses would be filled up with riches. And when he looked for loot, he questioned the ministers and elderly about many of the things that we see in his books and papers, such as about the *Vilahomas*, the temples, the statues, the *aclla* nuns, to see if there remained some trace of where he could learn if there were more silver and gold and more riches and goods. And anything that did not bear the scent of wealth he never cared to learn or ask about. Such was the case of the Indian monks in Peru, of whom, because of living in the barren wastelands as they used to live, Polo could not have any knowledge, nor even imagine that such a type of life existed. The existence of the virgin *acllas*, yes, because they were in populated areas and were like treasurers of the riches and wealth that were in the temples of the sun; and this is what he, along with the rest, sought for.

Thus, there were in Peru two types of religious. Some served the great Illa Tecce Viracocha, whom they believed to be the creator of the universe and of the sun and of the moon and of the stars and of humans.

When they first tried to become a *Huancaquilli* or *Uscavillullu* (these were the names they had), they lived in congregation to learn all that was needed. They were as if in a novitiate, which they used to call *Huamac*, and the novice himself was called by this name. Their primary duty was to pray to the great *Illa Tecce* and to the other gods for the king, for the people, for the kingdom, for the ministers, and for all their needs. And they lived on the communal income belonging to the house where they lived. They had a thousand lavations, taking blood from their veins with very sharp flints; they fasted many days of the year and even had their type of Lent. The manner of fasting was to eat roots and herbs and grains of corn, and to abstain from meat, from fish, suet, pepper, and other things that seemed to tend toward luxuries. They obeyed the one who was put in charge of them, and could not marry after they had decided to serve the gods in this life; and they promised to obey the great *Vilahoma* and his vicars and to be obedient to their elders, and loyal to their kings, and to never touch a woman in their life. Many of these *Huancaquilli* were offered as children and persevered in both their asceticism and in their virginity until old age.

They went about wanly, dressed in brown or in black, with very long cloaks and disheveled hair cut short about their ears like manes. They did not drink wine. When they were in a populated area, they went two by two or three by three and not in pairs, like monks, but one after the other. Many or most of them were eunuchs, whom they call *corasca*,[47] some of whom castrated themselves in reverence to their gods; others they castrated when they were boys so that they could serve in this manner of living.[48] When they went out in the streets and plazas, they attracted all of the people after them, who considered them as saints. And they, with pharisaical pride, publicly prayed for the Inga and for the people, so that they would be esteemed. They hit themselves with stones; they prostrated themselves. The devil appeared to them many times in various figures of men or of animals, and persuaded them to do a thousand crazy things, even making themselves bleed with lancets, with flints, thereby killing themselves, or throwing themselves off cliffs.

When they seemed to be firm in their intentions, progressing in this way of life and in penance, they went to the mountains or wastelands to live in solitude and strict penitence, with permission from their *Tocrico*, who was like a prelate of theirs. And there, in addition to *titoy* and *huñicuy*, which are chastity and obedience, which they had promised, they added other vows of *uscacuy*, beggary or poverty, and *villulluy*, the wretchedness and scorn of the poor beggar, and they kept these two things carefully. Because of this there were many of these solitaries in the mountains and ravines very far away from the roads. The people commonly called these men *Huancaquilli*, that is, disinherited and cast out from all wealth, and exiled; and at times it even happened that elderly female sorceresses went to enjoy such solitude in the mountains.

There they contemplated the sun, the moon, and the stars, and they worshipped them almost without ceasing. They did not lack for idols: the mountains, the river basins, the rocky crags served them as temples, as oratories and sanctuaries. Who doubts but that the devil appeared to them there more often than in the populated places? What care the devil takes so that the idolater and the idol's priest worship and attend to the idols ceaselessly by night and by day with their superstitions and lies. And when they convert to the Catholic faith, he gives them a lukewarm manner so that they barely can remember God once a week.

47. [In Quechua, *corasca* signifies an individual who habitually takes an hallucinogenic herb, *cora*. Although the exact role of hallucinogens in Inca rituals in unclear, there is little doubt that Andean shamans used psychotropic plants to induce trance states (see Sharon 1978, 23–33).]

48. [For more on the third gender in Inca Peru, see Horswell 2007.]

They used to sleep on the ground, eat roots, and drink cold water, flagellating themselves with well-knotted cords. Thus, like the ancient anchorites, they were often visited in ancient times by the faithful. He who had lost something precious went to them so that they could divine where it was or who had taken it. She who had a husband absent in the war or in the ocean would ask them if he would return healthy, or if he would die there. She who was about to give birth would send to ask them to pray to the queen of heaven—for thus they called the moon—so that she would give birth safely. Finally, the people went to them for all their needs. If they died, the other solitaries nearby buried them with great laments and superstitions.

Acllas, consecrated virgins

Pachacuti Inga, the seventh of that name, lord of Pacari Tampu, restored the empire of Cuzco, which had been lost through warfare and earlier epidemics.[49] Repairing the city and rebuilding it, he made a law that everyone must worship the sun after the great *Illa Tecce Viracocha*, and also the moon, who they said was the sister and wife of the sun, and the morning star, child of both and their messenger. And so that this worship would endure, he made his famous temple in Cuzco in honor of the sun, and the atrium, which was large, he adorned in honor of the moon. This temple was one that the succeeding kings repaired and enriched various times, because each one went adding his part. And the one who most distinguished it was Pachacuti IX, the last of the Pachacutis. Many serious Dominican and Franciscan friars affirm that all of the walls and the entire roof was covered and sheathed with sheets and plates of gold. Nothing remained in the interior of the temple that was not gold.

Pachacuti VII also installed two types of ministers for this temple, with sufficient income for their sustenance, so that in this way the worship of the sun and the moon would never cease. The first ministers were men chosen from the first and second and third types of

49. [In the Quito manuscript, as recorded by Montesinos, Pachacuti VII is credited with building a university in Paucari Tambo where the youth were instructed in *khipus* for the first time. According to the text, he worshipped Illa Tiçi Huiracocha and sent out messengers ordering people to give up the worship of local gods and animals and to cease the practice of male homosexual sodomy (Hyland 2007,130–31).]

priests that we described above, all of whom served, some by educating the public, others by prognosticating and declaring oracles, others by sacrificing.

He wanted the second type of minister to be chosen virgins, beautiful and of noble blood, called *acllas*, that is, elect and consecrated to the sun. And thus they were called *intip chinan* or *punchaopa chinan*; that is, maidservants of the sun, servants.of the daylight, but never *intip huarmin* or *punchaopa huarmin*, wives of the sun.

They had their type of novitiate, and the novices were called *huamac aclla*, recently elected, newly chosen. At a certain time of the year, magistrates whose job was to make sure that there was no shortage of young women in the temple went into the towns. There they ordered the publication of an edict or proclamation that any virgin who wished of her own free will to be an *aclla* in the Temple of the Sun could do so and should come to register. And if their parents wished to offer them to the gods, they should bring in the girls. And thus their parents or guardians handed over those who of their own free wills wished to go to the magistrate who had to bring them to the temple. And the truth is that for many Indians who had many daughters, this was a great relief, apart from the fact that in the temple the *acllas* were so cared for, with luxuries and adornments, that many young women willingly offered themselves for this.

They did not serve in turns, as some have thought, nor even less by force, as it appeared to Polo. Rather, being an *aclla* was very much to the liking of the virgins and their parents. And it was a matter of such esteem among them that parents would even beg for their daughters to be received, and would use intercessors to achieve this. This would not have been the case if the virgins had to be carried off by force whether their parents liked it or not. Apart from this, there was a maxim often repeated by the *mamaconas* who were in charge of them, that those who were brought by force never served well, nor did a well-done thing, nor remained. Once the maidens of a certain province or town were gathered, those who exceeded the others in beauty were chosen, and they were sent to Cuzco at the expense of the king and queen, accompanied by some old men and eunuchs, and they were given maids to serve them. The rest were placed in the temple of that province or town, each one according to the noble birth and abilities that she had. In this way, in all of the provinces where there were temples of the sun, maidens from the same nation were placed, or from provinces that were subject to that province. However, in the temple in Cuzco there were maidens of all nations, and especially three, that is, from Cuzco and its territory; from Chachapoyas; and from the nations of Pillco, now called Guanuco. I don't believe that there were any from the nations of Collas and its province.

I will describe the manner that was kept in Cuzco because from there it can be understood what was done in the other provinces. When the maidens entered the city to be received in the temple, they left to accompany the best of them, and they brought them before the king—and if he were absent, before those of his royal council, which they called *Hunu* (and the president was called *Capac Hunu*). And they examined them first about their age; whether they were at least at the age of puberty and, if so, were twelve years old or older. Secondly, whether they were legitimate; natural daughters were dispensed with easily, and bastards were never accepted. Third, if they had some marks in their face that made them ugly. Fourth, if they came of their own will and gladly, or if they came by force, or if they wished to marry in their own land. If they said that they came unhappily and wished to marry in their land or to stay with their parents until there was someone to marry, they gave them an unrestricted license to leave, and even punished him who had brought them by force. It was left to the *Mamaconas*, the matrons and superiors of the convent, to find out whether they were virgins. Once this was finished, the king or the president assigned each one sustenance and an income and a maid to serve them, whom they called *china*, and they were all sent to the great *Vilahoma*, and in his absence, to the *Hatun Villca*, who had his turn. The *Hatun Villca* examined them about almost the same things, and whether the *quichuchicuy*,[50] which were certain superstitions and sacrifices that were performed

50. [In the girls' puberty ritual, also called the *Quicuchicuy*, "the girls were required to fast for three days, eating nothing, and on the third day they were given a little raw maize. . . . [T]he girls were shut up in their houses, and on the fourth day, their mothers washed the girls and combed and braided their hair. Then the girls were dressed in elegant clothes with *ojotas* [sandals] of white wool. On this day the girls' relatives came to their house, and the girls came out to serve them food and drink. This feast lasted two days. Later the most important uncle of each girl gave her the name that she was to have permanently. . . . The uncle presented her with whatever he saw fit . . . and each of her other relatives and friends presented something to her with certain ceremonies" (Cobo 1990, 202–3).]

when the girl reached the age of puberty, had been done. If it had not been done, they waited until it could be done at their parents' hands if they were there, or by their guardians or caretakers or relatives. Once it was done, their hair was cut, leaving some hanks of hair on the forehead and temples. They covered their hair with a purple or dun-colored veil and dressed them with the dun-colored vestments of the novices, very modestly. And the *Vilahoma* exhorted them at length about what it was to be an *aclla* and that they should strive to serve the sun and the moon and the morning star very purely, because they were beautiful like them. And during the time of *hua-mac*, each one would see whether she wished to remain all of her life in the temple or not, and depending on what her heart wanted, thus she could do. Later they were handed over to those who governed and cared for them. And as there were many who were in the temple (because there were more than three thousand in Cuzco), novice mistresses were chosen, one for every ten girls, and these answered to a headmistress, and the headmistresses to the abbess or superior of the convent, and she to the *Villahoma* or *Hatun Villca*. Ancient and wise *Yana Villcas* were chosen also to see to what was needed for medicines and other things and to provide them.

The novitiate lasted three years, and in all of this time they taught the girls to spin, and to weave, and to embroider, to make precious wines, bread, and delicate foods, to manage their house and family and all of the things of their false religion, to decorate the temple and watch over the sacred fire, *Nina Villca*, and many other things.[51] The novices were kept apart from the older women. Although there were no keys or doors, because they did not use them, except for door curtains of cloth or canvas, so great was the submission and obedience of these *acllas* that the older ones never went among the novices nor the novices among the older ones, unless they had permission from the abbess or the head mistress. The abbess was usually the daughter of the king or of some great lord who descended from the royal lineage; the other superiors were also of very noble blood.

There are *quipos* that relate that some widowed queens and virgin princesses entered this convent of their own free will, to live in it

51. [Noting that "when women live together in isolation over long periods of time, their menstrual cycles tend to become synchronized," Urton has suggested that the *acllas'* menstrual cycles may have been observed to mark "nocturnal celestial cycles" (1981, 79).]

permanently, and that these royal women obeyed their *Mamaconas* (thus they called the superiors) with as much humility and submission as the most common. No princess, or infanta, or daughter of a great lord who entered there ever left the convent to marry anybody, because they held it as a great affront for a girl who had been consecrated to the sun to subject herself to any man. They also placed in this convent the young daughters of many leading persons so that they would learn to spin, weave, sew, cook, make wine, manage the household, and other necessary things; and these girls were among the novices, although they were not to become *acllas*. Once they had reached the age of eighteen, or were ready to marry, their parents took them out with the permission of the superior, who was distinct from the others, widowed and elderly, like a teacher of little girls. And if any of them wished to be an *aclla* and remain in the temple, she was accepted and the time she had been there served as her novitiate.

When the three-year novitiate was finished, the great *Vilahoma* came accompanied by the king or by the president. They seated themselves in the atrium of the temple, where there were aisles, and brought out all of the novices called *huamac*, who had finished three years of the novitiate, to examine them. Their novice mistresses and also the prefects who cared for them came out with them. And they asked the girls how that devotion and life seemed to them; whether they had decided to stay in the temple and be chosen *acllas* or *chinas* of the sun, that is, maidservants and *ñustas* of him and of the moon, that is, spouses of the sun and ladies of the moon, or if they wanted to marry; they should consider and decide this and state it there. And they were asked if they knew that if they married and fell into adultery, they would have to die according to the law; and if they decided to be *acllas* and fell into sexual sins, they would also die a cruel death. And that the law had determined not only this, but also that once a girl had been made an *aclla* and been accepted as such, she could not marry either in secret or in public, under the penalty of death for both the man and the *aclla* who did this. The novice mistresses responded for them, according to what they knew to be in the girls' hearts. And if they said that yes, they wished to marry, they were set apart. If they said that they wished to remain, they dressed them in white and put on them a garland of gold called *cori uincha*, and some precious shoes, and a white veil called *pampacuna*. And having performed certain sacrifices and supplications to the sun, along with other ceremonies, they brought them to the male eunuchs who cared for the convent. These eunuchs brought the girls to the one who was like an abbess, who, if she were a virgin, was called *Mama aclla* or *Aclla mamanchic*; if she were a widow, *Mamanchic*. *Mamacona* is the plural number, meaning many widowed superiors; *Aclla mamacona*, many virgin superiors.

Here these women were in the temple all of their lives. They wove fine cloth for the temple, for their gods, for the *Vilahoma*, and for the king and the queen and for their parents and brothers and sisters, if they had them, or for their guardians and caretakers. They used to go to visit the temples and sanctuaries that were in the town, and clean and decorate them; but each time they went, in pairs (and by no means alone), certain elderly women and their maids and two officers, who were guards of the temple and carried a lance in one hand and a bow with arrows, went with them. They could not leave without this accompaniment because, in addition to the fact that they were greatly esteemed throughout all the land, everyone took great care that they always remained untouched and pure. It seemed to the Peruvians that while these *acllas* were kept in a state of virginity, the gods would be very well disposed to the people. The principal duty of these women was to guard and watch over the fire for sacrifices, called *Nina villca*, sacred fire.

No other gentiles are known to have taken vows of perpetual virginity and kept them, other than the Peruvians with their *aclla* virgins. This was not because the devil, who taught this type of convent, was idle about chastity and virginal bodily purity like that which these *acllas* kept, but because by this route he wanted to teach, as he really taught, many superstitions and lies, many abuses in the affairs of idolatry.

No history or *quipo* is known to exist that states that any of these *aclla* virgins ever fell into the sins of the flesh. And when the Spaniards entered the land, they found some convents next to Cassamarca and Huaylas. Although the Spaniards thought they were witches, they later found out everything about what they were, and many of the women, receiving holy baptism, remained virgins, offering themselves newly as *acllas* of Our Lord Jesus Christ, while others fled to the wilds. The nuns of Cuzco did the same; more than two thousand of them were converted to the Lord, and most remained virgins until death. And others married recently baptized Indian men, and others fled to various parts. However, all or most of them came to become Christians, and those Indians who most flowered in devotion and modesty were these women.

Every year after the harvest, the *acllas* held a sumptuous banquet in Cuzco, and those who were very far away held one in the largest convent in their province. And here they renewed their homage and the vows that they had made to obey, first, the gods and their ministers, and then the Inga and his ministers. For this the king was pleased to be present (and in the lands where the king could not be, his viceroy, *tocrico*, attended), seated in an eminent place under a canopy, with his royal vestments and insignias, and the tassel of kingship. And the idols of *Illa Tecce Viracocha*, and of the sun, and of the moon, and of the morning star, and of lightning were present, each one in its altar scattered with gold and silver and precious stones and flowers, with their ministers and soothsayers and diviners. And the king's army and bodyguard, placed very much on their guard, were there; and the council and the president, the other magistrates and the great and principal lords, all placed according to their rank and age, and seated. And after them a large number of the people, who had gathered from various places to see the king and the festivities, and especially to see the virgins, all of whom, close up, were extremely beautiful. When the speeches and certain animal sacrifices, and the vows and the homage, and the kissing of the hands of the king and of the women of the realm, who were also on their platform under the same canopy, were finished, then the tables were brought out in this manner: for the king they put out a tall table higher than half of a *vara* [approximately a yard] or two *tercias*, all made of flowers and covered with a tablecloth of very white cotton, and the same for the queen, but her table was lower. And instantly the virgin *acllas* came out dressed in white and red, accompanied by many lords. Beginning with the king and the queen and the crown prince, they gave abundant food to everyone. And as there were many people, they went in good order and organization, fifty to each area, with their prelates and manservants, giving out also the wine that they had made of grains of corn. Finally, they took a small portion of bread like a round host but thick, and gave each portion to each person. And it was like an act of religion and idolatry to receive this bread and to eat all or part of it and to worship the idols. This bread was considered to be a great gift and guarded it as if it were a relic. And they called it *illai tanta*, divine bread, sacred bread. At other times they began the festival with this bread, as they desired and had planned.

Later the virgins took out all of the fine cloth that they had worked on all of that year, and offered the best and most unusual, of various colors and stitches, to the king and the queen and the crown prince and the princes and princesses, if there were any. Later they gave to each one of the lords and principal men and to their wives and children their precious garments, various headgear and shoes for men and women, sashes, wreathes, jewels, brooches, handbags, and many other things. The clothing was all from vicuña wool, which equals silk. For the rest of the people, they took out clothing made from common wool or from cotton, depending on the nation that was to receive it. With this act, the *acllas* gained more, because the lords and the people gave them great presents of livestock, land, gold, silver, wool, harvests, etc.

The day following this one was when they admitted the *acllas*, taking them out of the novitiate and incorporating them into the convent with the older women. The rest, who did not wish to remain but to marry instead, also left on this day. And, depending on their quality and nobility, those who were of high rank were married to the sons of lords, while plebeians married plebeians. Those who entered to be maids of these novices were from the plebeians and were given a husband of their rank. There was a very celebrated refrain that was very much put into use among the Peruvians, that said, "You should marry your equal," as if it were a law.

The king also took one or several of these women, not with the title of servant or maid, but to be a lady of the realm. And if he committed some sins there, it was not with all the women, nor all the time; nor did all the kings do this. The same can be understood about the Inga giving some of these women to other lords; he gave them to these lords to care for them as guardians and caretakers, and to marry them in their time. And if one or several of the lords dishonored them, not all did. Many were prohibited from marrying them, and watched over them with as much care as if they were their own daughters. And many chosen girls were given to their parents so that the parents could arrange their marriage according to their wishes. Moreover, it cannot be found in any *quipo* or history, ancient or modern, that any of these virgin novices who did not wish to remain in the temple were picked to be sacrificed and killed for the good of the people, or of the place, or from necessity. Nor can it be found that any died in this manner, but always to the contrary. Nor do I know where Polo[52] could have arrived at such an interpretation, unless it is that he heard it said that they sacrificed *pasñas* and *ñustas* and *acllas* and *huahuas;* but he did not understand the language of the Indians, that the lambs and sheep that were sacrificed in name of these *acllas* or of other young ladies were called *pasña, chusña,* and *ñusta,* and those in the name of the same *acllas* were also termed *acllas;* and the lamb was called *huahua,* child. And whoever does not pay heed to the tropes and metaphors that this language has will always say one thing for another and will make everyone who follows him fall into error.

The *acllas* were essential, inviolable. And if, when they walked along the street accompanied by their maids and guards, some delinquent came up to them, the police could not apprehend him, because the presence of the *acllas* was considered as sanctuary, as the temples are considered also for all of the delinquents who go there. Beyond this, according to their laws it was prohibited for them to marry; besides the very harsh penalty that existed, such a marriage would not be taken as valid. And whoever mistreated the *acllas* physically or verbally would be punished very severely. In the banquet that we describe above, there is no mention of the great *Vilahoma,* because he was never present at it, but he would send his gifts. Only at the distribution of the novices was he present, or his deputy, the *Hatun Villca,* whom some corruptly call *Appo panaca,* in order to say *aponaca,* the lords, in Aymara, or *apocuna,* in Quichua.

Superstitions

I do not believe that there have ever been gentiles as given to superstitions as the Peruvians; in some provinces superstitions were used more and in some less, but generally the entire kingdom had the same amount. Because, apart from that which concerns their false religion, their gods, their sacrifices and their temples, their sepulchers and oratories, and priests and sorcerers, they used to depend upon

52. The authors cited above, page 5, 6 [chapter on sacrifices], are against Polo, as are the common tradition of the Indians and their quipos.

superstitions from childhood, because they saw omens in all their acts and in their occupations, and in almost everything they found a mystery that indicated good or evil. The trembling of an eye; the ringing in an ear; stretching the body; coughing; sneezing; yawning; stepping with the right or left foot; stumbling over one's feet more with this one than with that one; the saliva going to the right or forcefully when they spit; encountering, after daybreak, the first man or woman with this or that look; seeing another person first, or the reverse; seeing animals, snakes, or insects fighting or mating; in all of these things they used to find evil or good omens. They used to say that the barking or howling of dogs signified brawls or deaths; the hooting of an owl, that someone within the house in which the bird sang would die; seeing the rainbow, that there would be fevers; pointing at it with a finger, that one's body would rot with abscesses or cancer.

For this protection the Peruvians, down to the little girls, used various types of good luck charms: in the grain of corn; in the cob of an ear of corn; in the saliva thrown into the palm of a hand; and in another thousand things. In the colored clouds of the morning sky they observed not only the quality of the weather, if it was airy, if rainy, if serene, but also omens and auguries. Finally, they were so given to these superstitions that in all their corporal acts, and in all things, they found omens to observe and to note.

Conversion of the Peruvian Indians to the Catholic faith

There have been three methods in Peru for Christianizing the natives. The first was by force and with violence, without having been preceded by any catechism or instruction. This occurred in Puna, Tumbez, Cassamarca, Pachacama, Lima, and other places, when the preachers were soldiers and the baptizers idiots. The baptized were brought in neck yokes and chains and bound, either made into a string of prisoners or into a pack, with the threat that if they did not raise their heads for baptism, they would sample the Spaniards' swords and guns. Of those who were baptized this way, first, they did not receive the grace of baptism; second, most of those Indians, it is understood, did not receive either the sacrament itself nor its character, because they clearly did not internally desire baptism,

although externally they seemed to consent to being baptized out
of fear that the Spaniards would kill them, as they had killed others
who clearly said they did not wish to become Christians. And it can
be seen that this is the truth, because these Indians later returned to
their superstitions, not considering themselves to be Christians, and
practicing the same as they did in ancient times. The Spanish soldiers
and citizens, as they revealed by their actions, did not try so much to
make the Indians Christian to save their souls as to work them for
the Spaniards' own interests and comforts. They pretended that they
baptized the Indians to unburden their consciences so that it wouldn't
seem that the Indian served them and paid tribute and worked for
the Spaniard and his children like a slave without getting any benefit.
And on the other hand, they allowed the Indians to practice all of
their gentile superstitions and vices, not trying to correct them, nor
did they observe Catholicism or teach them the faith throughout
the year. Concealing the Indians' lack of faith was very good for the
Spaniards' own comforts and interests; they claimed that trying
to have the Indians occupied in instruction and the reform of their
customs, even for one day, would cost the Spaniards too dearly and
would make them lose their estates. This attitude still endures to
this day in many parts of the kingdom, especially where there are
profits from mining, from working the land, from coca, from sweat-
shops in sugar mills, and from the other things in which the entire
Indian nation, particularly the commoners, are today occupied. The
Indians were made to resettle, and as they then either lived among
the Spaniards or were forced to come to the new cities, leaving their
towns, they learned many vices from the Spaniards that they had
not known. Or if they had known and been inclined toward them,
at least they did not commonly or publicly practice them because
of the strictness of their laws, which they carried out to the letter.
In those times, leaving aside everything that smacked of idolatry,
paganism, and superstition, the Spanish soldiers and citizens were
much more corrupt for their part in their customs and moral and
civil life than were the gentile Indians, as given to their amusements
as the Spanish were. Apart from stealing, robbing, causing damages
and injuries, swearing, blaspheming, renouncing God, murder among
even themselves, and many other evils, in matters of obscenity it was
so bad that everyone, from the captain down to the common soldier,
lived wickedly, some with five, some with ten, some with twelve

concubines, and all Indians. And all of the girls were taken either from their parents, who had kept them as maidens for marriage, or from their husbands. And to take away their scruples, they had them baptized without any catechism or preparation whatsoever. Once the baptism was done, they returned them to their houses and sins, and those girls who a little earlier had been gentile concubines became, on the same day of baptism, baptized and Christian concubines. And they also took boys from their parents to serve as procurers to call up one girl today and another girl tomorrow. Given that similar Indians, trained and baptized in such a manner and with such examples, were evil, full of vice and wickedness, is it surprising that the government of the Ingas, the rigor of their laws, and the execution of them ceased with the death of Don Juan Atahuallpa?[53] There did not remain anyone who could govern the Indians in civility and morality. How could they not give free rein to vices, having found the door open, because for a long time the Spanish who succeeded to the government did not try to curb immorality, preoccupied with their chaos and greed. And the Spanish, who were supposed to be the example of Christian virtues, were the most feeble and wicked, and the boldest in encouraging married women to leave their husbands and virgin daughters to leave their parents, giving themselves over to public lewdness. This is a thing that in all that had come before for more than two thousand years had never been seen in the kingdom of Peru. How could the Indians not be brutal and become barbarians without laws, when the situation, and even more the civil wars that followed, did not allow the evangelical or civil law to be conveyed to them, neither from Spain nor from the good laws of their ancestors? And in the end the Indians were left without law, without government, without a future. From such Indians like these, it must be understood, came what certain serious authors have written, saying that virginity among the Peruvians was not valued, nor did they wish to marry a woman who was a virgin because it seemed to them that she was not worth anyone else loving her.

That this cannot truthfully be said about the ancient Peruvians while the Ingas governed is seen very clearly by what has been written above about the Peruvian vestal virgins. The first and most important condition asked of them was their virginity, without

---

53. [Atahuallpa was executed in Cajamarca on July 25, 1533.]

which, according to their laws, none could be received, as the same authors admit. They dispensed with virginity only in the case of queens and great ladies who, widowed, wished to enter the convent. This concern with virginity is seen also in the death penalty that the laws imposed for rape and in the laws for forcing the rapist to marry the violated maiden, if she wished it, and not any other woman. This was seen also in the time of the Ingas in the great care that was taken for all types of maidens and young girls, since there were magistrates in charge of families and the education of boys and girls.

Moreover, this is also true for those Indians in these corrupt times of which we speak. If he who professed Christianity was the one who committed rapes and later gave these women to his servants who were Indians, telling them that he was giving them to honor them and that they should marry them, how many learned that it was an honor to take a woman violated by a Spaniard and to marry her? To what extent did the native lords and caciques learn to do the same with their vassals? What Christian teachings did they hear in all that time? Who told them that virginity is the highest state in the Church of God? What examples of virtue and decency came so that they could learn what is good? Thus it came about that, as some important persons (who later left Spain for the Indies) saw and learned what was happening, they thought that these were vices that came from ancient times. And as they imagined it, so they wrote, notwithstanding that they also knew about the corruption of the Spanish soldiers, the carelessness of the magistrates, and the upheaval of the civil wars among the Spaniards themselves, when they did not follow the law nor do anything good to serve the public welfare. Yet, with everything, there were those who excused the Spaniards or who hushed up their scandals and greatly animated the Indians. It must be understood that it is of these Indians who were baptized and instructed in this way that the various famous Councils of Lima speak when they describe how the Indians dig up the dead, taking them from the churches and carrying them to the mountains, where they practiced their ancient superstitions and sacrifices and evils, etc. But it is not understood to mean the Indians of today, who have forgotten all the ancient things. And if there are one or two who are apostates, is it any wonder, given that in Europe we see entire apostate kingdoms, and in Italy and Spain there is no shortage of those who have left the Catholic faith?

The second method of Christianizing the Indians was for those who of their own free will wanted to be Christians, because they were inspired by the holy example of some good friars or of some pious·secular Spaniard (there did not lack for these, but there were fewer than there could have been). But the Indians did not have anyone to teach the faith to them in their language. They contented themselves with saying the Our Father, the Hail Mary, and the Creed in Latin, putting up a high cross in public, and kneeling there in the mornings and at twilight. Friars were few, and those who did exist were busy founding houses and monasteries in the cities of the Spaniards, and in their communal prayer and other things. And thus they could not attend to the Indians, and if they did attend to them it was by means of interpreters who knew our Spanish Castilian language very badly; although, while the civil wars lasted, there was neither the former nor the latter. And since in those times it was the custom that the persons who went to minister to the Indians were commonly without voice—deprived of an active or a passive vote in elections in the religious community—there were very few who were inclined to go to the Indians, because it seemed like an affront. And if one went alone, he had an entire province under his care, without having the education or the languages for evangelization. And he would have to go to take care of forty or fifty or more towns, which one person alone cannot do. Because of this shortage, it came about that they put secular Spanish priests in Indian towns as Christian teachers, who knew neither the Indian languages, nor even Christian doctrine. For them, everything went to building their hacienda, working their Indians, collecting tributes from the Indian leaders, and giving the Indians blows with their fists. And as they found themselves free in the grazing fields, they gave themselves over to all liberties, without leaving a young girl or a married woman untouched.

With such a method of Christian instruction as this, the natives could not progress. Yet early on they became tepid and lost the good desires they had, because they never heard divine words to inspire them, nor saw a good example to incite them; moreover, the departure of the friars and their devotions helped many to lose their faith and give themselves over to vices. For many years they did not see a priest, and if they saw one, they never learned what it was to confess one's sins sacramentally, like a Catholic Christian, because the priest did not want to give himself so much work. It was enough for him to pass quickly through the town and collect his stipend, in whose payment he was very industrious. And it is a thing worth noting that in every matter concerning the interest or comfort of pleasures of the Spaniards, there was no lack of linguists, interpreters, efficiency and extreme measures for sumptuous buildings, monasteries, the working of the land, servile jobs, deals, contracts, tributes, sales taxes, taxes with the renowned names of the king, the royal treasury, the viceroy, the audience, the citizens, and the rest of the ministers for all the delights and luxuries that lords and ladies can imagine for their pleasures and for a thousand other things. Nor did the Indians lack the ability and quickness of wit to understand and to figure out and to carry out their tasks, although they were told by exterior signs as if to the deaf. Yet for preaching the Catholic faith and the glory of Our Lord Christ there was a shortage of interpreters and the ministers were lukewarm. And no sooner were the means found to be able to do these things, but the Indians were accused of being very slow and dull-witted and unable to learn anything that they had ever heard, or do any virtuous thing.

And this is, and has been, the fundamental complaint that those who have commented upon the Peruvians' little progress in Christianity have and have had. They expect that with the type of instruction we have described, the Indians should be as fervent as the primitive Church. Yet since this is greatly lacking, they complain that the Indians, although not taught, do not shine with virtue and holiness, which in the Spaniards who are taught does not shine. It is clear that the Indians would learn the things of Christ if they were taught, as they learn the things of the king because they are instructed. Is it possible that those who know all the royal decrees and sanctions concerning tributes and the royal treasury, for mines, communities, personal service, and other things, and know them by heart because they repeat them every day, would not at least learn the Creed and the Commandments with their brief declaration, if they repeated them and memorized them? Who has such knowledge of the king and of his power and majesty, and doesn't have it of the pope and of his authority and sovereign dignity?

It thus remains that even for these second types of Christians it is no wonder that in their Christianity they are weak and not fervent, and in their virtue they are inconstant and not persevering in their good desires and goals. And in their vices they are somewhat

excessive and dissolute and have gone back to resuscitate some of the
corrupt costumes that their elders had, such as lechery with common
women, intoxication, not respecting their parents and elders, and
other vices that they did not know in ancient times, such as perjury,
giving false testimony, stealing, being disagreeable, feeling weari-
ness and fastidiousness toward the things of God, coveting money,
not looking out for the common good, living in sin with women,
etiam [even] married ones, not forgiving injuries, being stubborn
and rebellious, etc. Nonetheless, with all this, in few or none have
we seen a lack of the faith they received, and especially among those
who received baptism in childhood. We have seen none sin flagrantly,
even with their enemies walking around with their eyes very alert
to catch them. In the Indian towns that are apart from the Spaniards,
two adulteries, theft, murders, cruel enmities are not found in an
entire year, although those who live among Spaniards fall into these
things frequently because they have the examples at hand. And if we
compare the one with the other, we find among the Spanish soldiers,
and among others who are called soldiers, more evils in one month
than among the Indians in one year; the cities of Lima, Mexico City,
Havana, and others are witnesses to this. Yet these Indians do not
deserve any excuse because of this, their critics say, but rather repri-
mands, since they could progress in the righteousness they feel from
the evangelical law, and separate themselves from evil people and not
become one with them.

The third way in which the Peruvians entered into Christianity was for Indians who not only wanted baptism of their own free
will for themselves and their children and their wives, but who had
the good fortune to find someone to teach them and to inspire them
to a fervor for the faith and for the love of God through their good
example. And if perhaps they lacked someone to teach them, they
looked for ways to learn what they were obliged to, and taught it to
their children. And as an Indian who does what he should and ought
never lacks for God, he sent them some illustrious ecclesiastical
clergy and friars, who with great and praiseworthy efforts learned
the language of the land. And these, putting off all the honors of the
world and the comments of those who were so averse to the Indians,
concerned themselves with publicly preaching the gospel, going from
town to town getting rid of idolatry, not only from the exterior self,
like the first and second type of missionaries who did not know the

language, but also from the heart and will. In this way they did not need to go to the idols and break them and destroy ancient altars and shrines, because the Indians themselves turned all the idols and altars that there were into fragments and ashes. And they uncovered and destroyed those idols and altars that were hidden. The Indians themselves called attention to all the mountains and springs and other natural things that the ancients venerated so that the preachers knew about them and would preach against such evil superstitions. From these Indians we know all of the things that have been referred to above, and more things that are not spoken of, because the Indians, hating such evil things, have not only cast them out of their hearts entirely, but have revealed them so that the priests will be aware of them.

The Dominican friars have greatly distinguished themselves in this work, always proceeding with great prudence and discretion, along with holiness and virtue. Of these, Friar Cristóbal López was a holy man worthy of eternal memory; also Friar Domingo de Santo Tomás and others.[54] In the order of Saint Francis there were not as many interpreters and linguists, but those who consecrated themselves to the good of the natives did all they should. Among the Augustinians (although they arrived later) there was no shortage of good laborers, particularly one who not only worked but wrote in the language for the benefit of those who would come later.

The secular clergy could not go among the Indians if they did not have large stipends. However, there were some who devoted themselves to the apostolic life, such as Machin de Deva, Gregorio de Montalvo, Cristóbal de Molina, Juan de Pantaleón (the latter was hanged by the rebel Gonzalo Pizarro because he persuaded Indians to the service of the king), and two or three others who did very useful works. And as things went in those times, these friars and priests did not do a small thing in looking out for the Indians, but rather a heroic and heavenly act, full of humility and contempt for the world, full of the love of God and of one's neighbor, and a perpetual mortification. In those days it was considered as a dishonor and a great demotion to go to and preach to the natives, as today it is considered if an important nobleman went to speak to and converse with rogues

54. [A Spanish Dominican (1499–1570) who compiled the first Quechua grammar (Domingo de Santo Tomas 1560).]

or petty thieves. And to order imperfect friars to go to the Indians was like telling them to go to the galleys. In this way it was necessary that their work, which is heavenly, had to come from the heart. But it was God's providence that there were both forced missionaries and voluntary missionaries in order to see the difference.

For more than thirty years, all of these preachers attended only to preaching to the natives and of the sacraments, they offered the Indians only baptism and marriage. And as the missionaries were few and the Indians without number, they could not go to baptize all the provinces and towns, and thus many of the second type of conversion were lost. This we saw above, because if in so much time they did not even know the name of Jesus Christ Our Lord, how much less could they have learned the mysteries of the faith? Nor were they helped by the sacraments, nor inspired to virtuous things. And although they saw the good examples of the good preachers, with everything, the evils of the other missionaries dragged them down and carried them to their level, in such a way that they practiced vices, as has been said already. Those of the third manner of conversion were also endangered by the shortage that existed of anyone to hear their confessions, because at that time it was considered a miracle for some priest to apply himself to hearing the confessions of Indians. And if, for their sins, some of the less fervent ministers went to confess them, it would have been better if they hadn't. Because as they dispatched one hundred and fifty every day, those who went were not truly shriven, nor did the minister perform his duty, for one thing because of haste, and for another because the minister barely knew the language, and for another because he did not prepare them first by explaining to them how they must receive the sacrament. For more than thirty-eight years it was neither preached to nor suggested to the Indians that it was necessary to receive the holiness of the Eucharist, nor what it was, nor even the holy sacrifice of the Mass, and much less the other Sacraments.

And it was pitiful to see the tears of the natives who complained that they were not taught in the way that the Spaniards were taught, etc. In this manner, the Indians generally knew only baptism and marriage, and only when there was the practice and habit of receiving them. During lessons in Christian doctrine, there was only one Indian out of a thousand who knew anything because he had gotten some benefit from the good missionaries we have described.

God heard the petitions and tears of the Indians and sent them the Society of Jesus in the year 1568. That same year in the month of September, and much more through January of the following year of '69, the Jesuits got off to such a good start with their preaching and good example that the natives themselves were surprised at seeing such a notable change, a fervor and devotion never seen before and such a large concourse of Indians; never had so many people been seen in Lima. The archbishop Don Hierónimo de Loaisa cried with pleasure each time he saw the procession of innumerable Indians pass through the streets on Sundays and feast days. He rejoiced at the practice of confession that began then with the Indians. And it was seen clearly and manifestly that the fault had not been with the watch but with the watchmaker, since the Indians, finding the door open for what they desired, rushed to it then. The devil was greatly grieved at so much goodness and later invented a terrible obstruction, because God thus allowed the constancy of the new missionary priests and the true devotion of those newly converted to be known.

Jealous and relentless people wished to take advantage of this circumstance and of the good work of the Society to command that, since there were so many Indians, they should serve everyone and more should be brought from the mountains where they had come from. And although the pious resisted this, the impious ones tried harder, bringing up insolent reasons: among others, that such devotion showed that the Indians were becoming lazy and wouldn't work in the Spaniards' estates; that the Indians already possessed and had been given sufficient Christian instruction until then; that why were new types of processions and devotions and confessions necessary when they were more cumbersome; that the Indians wanted this and they became lazy and cunning. In this way the impious were pained that the Indians were thus being healed, and they desired that what they themselves did not want to receive out of malice, the Indians didn't get either. With all this, many Indians fled so that they wouldn't be forced to provide personal service, although they never left off their devotion, because there in their homelands they were on the lookout, waiting for the Jesuits to be there or to pass through their area. Those who remained in the city suffered a lot, although they did not abandon what they had begun. Finally, an agreement was made to found the community of Santiago, called Cercado, close to Lima, where the Indians were gathered together and taught

Christian doctrine by those of the Society. This done, an infinite
number died with the move to the place; those in charge took other
Indians, who did not rejoice in so much "happiness." Finally, a large
number remained, who until now have persevered with so much
virtue, decency, and devotion that it is something to admire. With
their own alms and work, without anyone's help, they have built the
church of Saint Blas, which was converted later into a hospital. They
have built the church of Saint Santiago, which in loveliness, beauty,
and decorations exceeds many of the churches of Lima. The altar's
oratory for the tabernacle of the Most Holy Sacrament; the finery
of the ministers who serve there; the music for the divine office, not
only of voices but also of different instruments and of the guitar-like
vihuelas; the illustrious and sumptuous ceremony with which they
take the Holiest Sacrament to sick Indians; the confraternity that has
been instituted in its honor, in which are incorporated the Confraternity of Our Lady and of the True Cross and of the souls in purgatory;
the usefulness and comfort of this confraternity; the cures and medicines and provisions and safeguards of the hospital; the assistance for
the poor and orphaned; the sustenance of the priests who live there
to teach them; the continual alms that are given there, not only to
their spiritual fathers, but also to the house of probation that is there;
all these things come from the Indians and not from others. Apart
from this, these same Indians, through their alms, help the hospitals
and confraternities and needs of the poor of Lima.

Given all this, who will say that it is feigned, or who will take this
in a bad sense? What more could the most ancient Christian worship-
pers do exteriorly? Well, and what is clear is that all of this goodness has come from their frequency in confessing and in receiving
the Most Blessed Sacrament on the major and solemn feasts; where
is this seen better than in the Cercado? There are communities of
Indians near there that have the same desires and longing, and even
preparations, but *non est qui frangat panem eis* [there is no one who
may break bread for them]. Before this, the Jesuits had been reprimanded from the pulpits because they shared these divine Sacraments with the Indians. More than twenty-four sermons were given
about the apparent reasons why the secular priests thought it was
the pure truth that the Jesuits were wrong to do this. Because of this
all of the secular clergy decided to follow such preachers, bringing
about, in consequence, some frailties and falls of Indians, as if there

had never been such faults also among the ministers themselves. The friars wished to go forward with what they had done until then, of generally not hearing confessions from Indians, except in unusual cases, and much less giving them the Most Blessed Sacrament of the Eucharist. And because they never asked the Indians some day if they knew they could receive it, having a proper disposition and preparation, they resolved never to attempt this matter.

Yet the Jesuits, governed by the true spirit of the Catholic Church, went forward with this work with considerable prudence and discretion. If in the Cercado of Lima and among the rest of the devout Indian people who live in the city the Jesuits have done everything that has been described and many more things that haven't been described, it was even more admirable what they did and achieved in Cuzco, assisted by divine grace. And they were held in such great esteem that the enemies of virtue, for their part, greatly and more grievously obstructed and persecuted them, while among the natives there was greater faith and constancy. The methods that the Society of Jesus used were patience, humility, obedience, charity, fervent prayer, and rushing to their ministries with hearts on fire, without making excuses for sweat, labor, hunger, without fearing persecution. The ministries were to preach, to hear confessions and to give communion, to go to the sick, to prisoners, to hospitals, to children and to the rough and coarse, to find a way to help the needs of the poor, to resolve quarrels and enmities, and to avoid public sins. Their method of preaching was new to the Indians and never used until then, such as adorning the pulpit with silk; making the worship and the beginning of the sermon as if for a Christian listener, and explaining that each one of those who were there had a sovereign angel in heaven as a servant; taking the authorities on Holy Scripture in the Latin language and then interpreting them faithfully in the native language, because thus they will reverence the divine word; customarily preaching to them on historical themes because they enjoy this greatly, and taking from the historical narrative quotes and exclamations, either loving and tender, provoking penitence and reform, or terrible and frightening, provoking a divine fear and turning away from vice; having processions; honoring the Indians according to their abilities and duties and recounting saints' lives and discussing things about virtue in particular conversations; composing lyrics to the divine in their language and making children sing them in front of the Indians, so that thus they forget the ancient songs and by means of music they are taught the Articles of the faith and the Commandments and the Sacraments and the Works of Charity.

So great were the fruit and benefits that they took from here, the very stones of Cusco declared it; although men may hush it up or deny it out of malice or forgetfulness, the stones will proclaim it.[55] Other friars, who enjoyed the great generosity in their alms, said that they saw a palpable reform and perseverance, although some of them made fun of and laughed heartily at the Society for two things:[56] the first, how as newbies and tenderfoots the Jesuits preached and worked, without being aware that they were throwing water into a sieve, and that the great devotion or hypocrisy of the Indians would be like a newly grafted twig, three days on the wall until it dies. And to shame those of the Society, or to make them give up their ideas, they went about with great diligence, inquiring if one of those who went to hear our sermons had fallen into any sin, and even if it were only carelessly or lewdly making eyes at someone, they recriminated him and laid down the law. Because of this the secular priests were encouraged not only to make inquiries about this itself, but also about whether it were known or had been heard said that any Indian, whoever it may be (because for this they made took as a rule that all of the province, without any exception, had enjoyed the teaching of the Society), had fallen into any lewdness or drunkenness. And they made such a big deal out of it and upbraided him so much, that you wanted to plug your ears. "Look," they would say, "the sermons of the Theatines that the Indians come to stay for, it's too much preaching to the Indians; it would be better to throw them into the mines and have them work for us." And there was a malicious soldier who had solicited a native woman from the land, who had never heard of nor seen the priests of the Society, and offended God with her; later, another day, he insulted her publicly, saying that she was evil and perverse, and blaming the preaching of the Fathers. And although

55. [This is meant to evoke the noisy cheers for joy when Christ entered Jerusalem. When the Pharisees asked Christ to quiet his followers, he responded, "If they were to keep silence, I tell you the very stones would cry out" (Luke 19:40 [New American Bible]). It may also reflect Andean beliefs that sacred stones (*huacas*) can speak.]

56. [Valera is stating that some friars mocked the Jesuits for (1) their seemingly naive belief in the faith of their Indian converts and (2) their style of preaching, described in the previous passage.]

the aforementioned friars laughed, the second thing—the manner of preaching that the Fathers of the Society had—set them into
a great uproar, as was stated above. Yet, with everything, as time
passed, they came to realize and they took back what they had said
about their first and second criticisms of the Jesuits and began to
help courageously, considering the missionary work now to be an
honor, which until then they had taken as a dishonor. Realizing that
the most distinguished members of the Society valued working with
Indians, there was no reason for them therefore to deprecate Indians.
And thus they began to preach to the Indians and began using the
style and method of the Society, hearing confessions from everyone
whom the teachings of the Society had humbled. Because there were
so many thousands who came, and every day new people came, the
Jesuits could not attend to everyone, even if there were twenty or
thirty confessors; and the other priests intervened because thus they
were inspired to help them. In this the Dominicans greatly distinguished themselves, and in nothing did they turn away from our
spirit and method of proceeding. The Mercedarians also did a great
deal with their sermons and some of their confessors. The Franciscans
did not have linguists then, nor did the Augustinians, but later when
they did, they helped to the great benefit of the Indians.

The devil, seeing that his machinations had been destroyed,
invented others. The bishop became so irritated and angry that the
Jesuits had such copious fruit among the Indians in his city and
diocese that he incited the vicar-general and vicars and curates—or to
state it better, they incited him—to hinder the Fathers' works. They
spread the rumor that, instead of preaching and hearing confessions,
the Jesuits wanted to take over all of the offerings in the parishes and
the towns and even, perhaps, in the entire diocese. Because of this,
the bishop ruled, under the penalty of major excommunication *latae
sententiae* [automatic, by the force of the law itself], that no clergy or
curate allow the Jesuits into their churches or towns, either to preach
or to hear confessions or for anything. The caciques and native lords
were under the penalty of one hundred pesos, and the rest a penalty of one hundred lashes and cutting their hair, that they not go
to confession with the said Fathers nor listen to any word of theirs.
Because of this they did terrible things; they flogged many, men as
well as women, and insulted them publicly, and imposed all manner
of imprisonment and exile and whatever other penalties that they

could; only murder was not allowed to them. But their intention was not fulfilled because the number of those who tried to reform grew to such an extent that they themselves were accused and known not to be going down a good road. Additionally, the royal magistrates took the side of defending the Indians and the Jesuits.

This devotion and reformation could not be better proven than by seeing that it continues until this very day with the same tenacity and to such an extreme. Almost this same manner, fervor, and devotion have existed and exist in Arequipa, Juli, Chuquiabo, Chuquisaca, Potosi, Tucuman, Chile, and especially Quito. The Jesuits have made two missions to Chachapoyas and Guanaco,[57] and the reform that occurred then continues now with great fruitfulness, although it is more than twelve years since the Society has gone to those parts. I will not speak of the great hindrances and impediments that daily labor and oppression have given and continue to give to the Indians; the many tributes and taxes that they have imposed on them, and more every year; the aggravations and vexations that they receive from the hands of the nearby and the faraway magistrates and their partisans; the horrible servitude that has come, for no reason but that they are Christians, and the overwhelming poverty that they have, not even being able to take care of raising their children and their houses because they do not have the space to attend to their salvation; the enmity of the secular priests toward them because the ecclesiastics attend to their instruction and defense; I do not say any of this because it would be lengthy to recount. But we see that even with so many burdens and loads (that with the smallest part of these many Spaniards would fall down, not only in virtue but in the loyalty that they owe to their king), the Indians are firm in their intentions, and in the midst of their labor and pain they embrace Christ. And meanwhile, the more grievances and hindrances and persecutions they suffer, the greater their firmness and rootedness in the faith. It is true that from their deciding truly to embrace Christ, torture and death will not suffice to separate them from him, as has been seen and experienced by many, who have allowed themselves to be killed by the hands of the Spaniards in order not to offend the Lord. And as Our Lord has permitted that in every place where there

57.   [The first mission to Chachapoyas and Guanaco was in 1576, the second in 1582.]

are gentiles who convert, there is someone who spiritually tests the newly converted for their greater advantage, as has been seen in Europe, Asia, and Africa, so he has allowed the Indian Christians to be likewise tested. And as there are no gentiles or heretics to martyr them, he has allowed certain Spaniards to serve as persecutors, mistreating them, harassing them, and injuring them. The magistrates fill this measure of molestations and injuries to the brim with their excessive tributes and impositions, such that the Indians are thereby tested and become rooted in the faith and seek for God in their tribulations and tears, as they do with great benefit and fruitfulness.

The first clue to the identity of the author as Valera is the unique information provided in the text about Blas Valera's father, Luis. The text states, "Authors are all of those already mentioned, but in particular Francisco de Chaves, of Jerez, who was a great friend of Tito Atauchi, brother of King Atahuallpa; who not only was informed about a thousand things, but who saw with his own eyes that which here is said, and wrote an extensive account that he left in the power of his friend and kinsman Luis Valera, and the latter gave it to Diego de Olivares." No other chronicle mentions a history written by Francisco de Chaves,[1] nor is there any other record that Chaves was the friend and relative of Luis Valera, with whom Chaves left his history. Most scholars believe that Luis's son Blas was the most likely source for this information. Moreover, this passage states that Chaves was the "great friend" of Tito Atauchi, Atahuallpa's brother. The only other text to comment on the friendship of these two men is a work by Blas Valera, known as his Vocabulary. Although this work is lost, Anello Oliva quotes passages from it in several places in his own history of the Incas. One entry reproduced from Valera explains how Tito Atauchi and Chaves made a peace treaty soon after Atahuallpa's execution, and that the two men were great friends (Anello Oliva 1998, 141–42). As Chaves's kinsman, Blas Valera would have known about the relationship between Tito Atauchi and Chaves, and

---

1. The so-called Naples documents, recently discovered in the private library of Clara Miccinelli, contain a brief letter allegedly written by Francisco de Chaves. This letter cannot be the same text as that referred to in the *Account of the Ancient Customs*. According to the *Account*, Chaves's text stated that there had never been human sacrifices among the Indians; however, the purported Chaves letter in the Naples materials never discusses whether the ancient Andeans practiced human sacrifice, and makes no statement of any kind about Andean religion or ritual practices (Laurencich Minelli 2005, 427–48).

is the most probable source for the information about Chaves in the *Account*.

The numerous, repeated correspondences between information in the *Account* and in the remaining fragments of Valera's writings have also led scholars to conclude that Valera composed the anonymous text. Much of this corresponding information can be found only in the *Account* and the writings of Valera. For example, the *Account* and the portions of Valera saved by Garcilaso share the same bibliography, including authors not mentioned in any other chronicle, such as Juan de Oliva, Falconio Aragonés, Diego de Olivares, and Franciscan Marcos Jofre (Hyland 2003, 85).

Another important series of correspondences between the *Account* and the writings of Valera concerns the pre-Inca kings of Peru. In the *Account*, the author claims that the first ruler of Peru was Pirua Pacaric Capac, not the Inca Manco Capac, as stated by other chroniclers. Among Pirua's successors, the text continues, was a ruler known as Pachacuti VII, the lord of Parcaritambu. The text also states that the Inca emperor Yupanqui, who bore the name Pachacuti, was the ninth emperor with that name. This unusual version of the pre-Inca kings is found in only one other colonial manuscript, the Quito Manuscript preserved by Fernando de Montesinos (see Hyland 2007). The Quito Manuscript presents a chronology of ninety-three pre-Inca rulers, beginning with Pirua Pacaric Manco and including eight pre-Inca kings who bore the honorific title of Pachacuti. Besides the *Account*, only one other text includes any of the royal names from the Quito Manuscript's chronology: Valera's Vocabulary, quoted by Anello Oliva. The kings Capac Raymi Amauta, Capac Yupanqui Amauta and Cuis Manco, all mentioned by Valera in the Vocabulary, are also part of the pre-Inca history of the Quito Manuscript; apart from the Quito Manuscript, Valera is the only chronicler known to adhere to this unusual pre-Inca history of Peru (for more on the relationship between Valera and the Quito Manuscript, see Hyland 2007, 65–67).

Another example of the correspondences between the writer of the *Account* and Valera, as quoted by Garcilaso, is their statements about human sacrifice in the Inca empire. The author of the *Account* and Valera, as cited by Garcilaso, are the only writers to argue that the Incas never practiced human sacrifice. Moreover, both texts agree that the chronicler Polo de Ondegardo was mistaken in his conclusion that the Incas ritually sacrificed human beings (Garcilaso de la Vega 1987, 92). Elsewhere in his work, Garcilaso explains in some detail that Valera, unlike most chroniclers, was favorable to the Inca Atahuallpa, rather than to Atahuallpa's half-brother Huascar, who also had claimed the Inca throne (592–93). We see that the author of the *Account* was also a partisan of Atahuallpa, stating that "the government of the Incas ceased with the death of Don Juan Atahuallpa." Only a supporter of Atahuallpa would have described him in that manner. Moreover, the *Account* refers to the slain emperor's baptismal name as Juan, rather than the more commonly used Francisco; Valera's Vocabulary likewise asserts that Atahuallpa was baptized Juan (Anello Oliva 1998, 107–8).

It is sometimes argued that the differing explanations for the name "Peru" found in the *Account* and in the citations from Valera in Garcilaso demonstrate that Valera could not have written the *Account*. These differences between the two explanations are not, however, as clear-cut as they may appear. In Garcilaso's excerpts from Valera, two explanations for the name of Peru are provided: (1) that it is from the word *Pelu*, which means "river," or (2) that is derived from the Quechua word *Pirua*, which means "granary." As the text states:

> The name *pelú* is a word that means "a river" among the barbarous Indians who dwell between Panama and Guayaquil. It is also from the name of a certain island, *Pelua* or *Pelú*. As the first Spanish conquerors sailed from Panama and reached these parts before the rest, the name *Peru* or *Pelua* pleased them so much that they applied it to anything they found as though it had meant something grand and noteworthy, and so they called the empire of the Incas *Peru*. . . . Many also affirm that this word is derived from *pirua*, a term of the Quechuas of Cuzco, meaning a granary for storing crops. I am quite willing to accept this opinion because the Indians of that kingdom do have a great many granaries for storing their crops. (Garcilaso de la Vega 1987, 19–20)

In the *Account*, the author writes that the land took the name of Peru from the word *Pirua*, which refers to the god worshipped by Pirua, the first inhabitant of the land. However, he goes on to explain that the God Pirua (associated with the planet Jupiter) was the guardian of "their granaries, their treasures, and their storerooms; because of this they called the most remarkable ears of corn or those that were first harvested, and the repositories that they kept in their homes to guard their treasures and clothes, dishes, and weapons, *Pirua*." Both texts, therefore, suggest that the name "Peru" derived from the term *pirua*, meaning granary or treasury. The differences in this matter between the *Account* and Valera as he is quoted by Garcilaso are more apparent than real.

The noted Peruvianist Jiménez de la Espada never accepted Valera as the author of the *Account* because he believed the text to postdate Valera's death in 1597. The *Account* describes in detail the Jesuit community of Santiago del Cercado, which Jiménez mistakenly believed to have been founded in 1616 or 1617. However, documents from the Harkness Library clearly show that El Cercado was established in the early 1570s (Harkness 1568, fol. 852r). The Jesuit Provincial Catalogs published by Antonio de Egaña reveal that Valera actually served as a priest in El Cercado in 1573 (*Monumenta peruana* 1966–86, 1:706; for an extended discussion of Valera's residency in El Cercado, see Hyland 2003, 47–52).

Occasionally, other Jesuits are suggested as possible authors of the *Account*. José Durand, for example, proposed that the Spaniard Luis López wrote the manuscript (Durand 1961). Rejecting Valera as the author on the questionable grounds that a mestizo would have been psychologically unable to appreciate his Indian heritage, Durand states that López's writings show López to have been the author. López was a Spanish Jesuit in Peru who was arrested by the Spanish Inquisition for the brutal rape of María Pizarro. After his arrest, Inquisitors discovered among the priest's papers a manuscript that criticized the Viceroy for Spanish abuses of the Indians (López 1889). Because López was highly critical of Spanish policy in the Andes, Durand argues that he was a likely author of the *Account*. However, many other aspects of López's letters contradict statements in the *Account*. For example, whereas the *Account* highly praises the faith of the Christian Indian converts, López has nothing but contempt for the Christianity of the native Peruvians. He writes that the Indians are "so inconstant and have such evil customs in their idolatries, drinking and concubines" that it would need great perseverance to turn them from their evil habits. Elsewhere, he refers to

Andean Indians as "vicious" and "embittered" (*Monumenta peruana* 1966–86, 1:361–71, 324–36); it seems highly unlikely that he wrote the *Account*, which praises native culture as a firm foundation for the Christian faith.

Throughout the *Account* are details that correspond to Valera's biography. For example, a repeatedly cited source of information is Sebastian de Quispe Nina Villca, the head *kuraka* (native leader) of the community of Huarochiri, where the Jesuits had a short-lived mission. Valera, one of the seven Jesuits in the mission (two of whom died during the Jesuits' time there), was the only native Quechua speaker among them (Hyland 2003, 38–52). Ninavillca's support was crucial to the Jesuits' efforts in Huarochiri (see *Monumenta peruana* 1966–86, 1:422), and Valera, who would have served as a translator in the Jesuits' dealings with him, would have known him well. Likewise, the text contains a lengthy description of Santiago el Cercado, where Valera served as at first as a lay brother and then as a priest (Hyland 2003, 47–52). Garcilaso tells us that Valera analyzed Native American religion in terms of Marcus Terentius Varro's (116 BC–27 BC) classification of paganism (Garcilaso de la Vega 1987, 81–83); in fact, the *Account*, unlike any other colonial text about native Andean religion, is organized according to Varro's typologies as well. As stated above, a majority of Andean scholars who have made detailed studies of this issue have concluded that Valera was the author of this text; the analysis of Valera's life and extant writings appears to bear out this attribution.

GLOSSARY OF QUECHUA TERMS

Based primarily on the dictionaries of Antonio Ricardo (1586) and Diego
Gonzalez Holguín (1608).

aclla	women who were dedicated to the sun or other deities
amaro	serpent
amauta	wise, prudent
anta	tapir
apachita	hills, piles of stones that the Indians worship
apocuna	great, rich, and powerful lords
aspai (also aspay)	to sacrifice a type of food (Ricardo, *aspacacuni*)
aucayoc	soldier, warrior, enemy, traitor
cancha	corral or patio
capac	king, rich, powerful, illustrious
Catuilla	related to the shrine of Catequilla in Huamachuco
chasca	disheveled; *chasca coyllur:* morning or evening star
chimpu	red clouds either around the sun or the moon
chinan	maidservant; any female animal
chucu	cap, hat, or skullcap of the Indians
chusña	a very tiny nose, or the person who has such a nose
coca	sacred herb from which cocaine is derived
cocuy	to offer
corasca	he who becomes intoxicated by herbs, from *cora*, "the evil herb that intoxicates"
cori	the metal gold
coya	queen, princess
çupay	demon, phantom, a person's shadow
cuy	guinea pig
guacamayas	a type of parrot
guadoi	José de Acosta wrote that after confession, the native Peruvians "also used these ritual baths, in a ceremony very similar to the one the Moors use, which they call *guadoi* and the Indians call *opacuna*" (Acosta 2002, 306).

hahua pacha	time, land, or place above or outside
hamurpa	examination; from *hamurpayani*, to consider attentively
harpay (also arpai)	a sacrifice of blood
hatun	something big or grand
haucha	a cruel, angry man
hayhuay	to touch something with the hand
huaca	idol or shrine
huacaylla	to make someone cry
huahua	what a mother calls her son or daughter
huamac	something new in the land, or something recently introduced
huaminca	adventurous in war; strong and brave
huampar	something decorated with triangles
huanaco	guanaco, Andean camelid
huancaquilli	native Andean hermit; possibly from *huancar*, tamborine
huaoque (also hauque)	brother (of a man)
huapil (also huipil)	overshirt (Mayan word from Central America)
huarmi	woman
huaspai	see *aspai*
huatuc (also huatu)	sorceror, diviner
humu	sorceror
huñicuy	to concede, to say yes
hunu	thousand
ichuris	confessor (Aymara)
illa	brilliant, shining
intip	of the sun
llama	llama, Andean camelid
mamacona	the matrons or ladies of illustrious lineage
mollo	seashells sacrificed by the Indians (*Spondylus*)
nacac	he who cuts open an animal, cuts its throat, quarters it
nina	fire, light
ñusta	princess or lady of illustrious blood
orcos (1)	male animal
orcos (2)	var. of *urcu* (2)
osno	outdoor altar
opacuna	washing the face
pacaric	the beginning
paco	a certain type of livestock; a reddish-brown animal
pampacuna	a kerchief or cloth that the Indian women wear on their head or as a veil
pasña	little girl, lass, maidservant
pirua	granary and a certain type of ear of corn that they have as an idol

pucyu	fountain, spring of water
punchao	day
quichuchicuy	to have celebrations for the first time a woman menstruates
quipo	an account by knots
quispi	something transparent like glass, crystal, etc.
runa	a person, a man or a woman
sayri	tobacco
tampu	roadside inn or hostelry
tanta	wheat bread or cornbread
tecce	origin, beginning, foundation, base
titoy	to give generously
tocapu	needlework which is embroidered or knitted or on cups [*kero*], boards, etc.
tocrico	he who governs or summons people
tomariy	to encircle or surround
urcu (1)	mountain
urcu (2)	var. of *orcos (1)*
uscacuy	to beg
utirayay	to act crazy
vila	he who refers, says, denounces, announces
Vilahoma	high priest of the sun
villca	idol or priest of an idol
villulluy	miserable
Viracocha	god worshipped by the Indians worshipped, a divine thing
yana villcas	subordinate priests
yuyac	he who is thinking or imagining something

Manuscripts

Archivo Histórico Nacional, Madrid (AHN)

1579–80. Proceso contra Fray Melchior Hernandez. AHN Inquisición, Libro 1027, fols. 77–78r.

1580a. Procesa contra Oxnam. Lima. March. Inquisición, libro 1027, fols. 107ab, 143a.

1580–81a. Procesos pendientes. Lima, April 1580–April 1581. Inquisición, libro 1027, fols. 69b, 118a–125b, 172b–173a.

1580–81b. Procesos pendientes, Lima, April 1580–April 1581. Inquisición, libro 1027, fols. 126b, 161b–162a.

1581–82a. Relación de negocios sentenciados e determinados. Lima, April 1581–February 1582. Inquisición, libro 1027, fols. 195a–197a.

1581–82b. Juicio contra Luis López, S.J., Lima, October 1581–March 1582. Inquisición, legajo 1654, exp. 14.

1595. Proceso contra Ricardo Haquines Lima, November 4. Inquisición, libro 1036, fol. 122a.

N.d.a. Proceso contra Miguel de Fuentes, S.J., Lima, Inquisición, libro 1027, fol. 195ab.

N.d.b. Juicio Miguel de Fuentes, S.J., Lima, Inquisición, legajo 1647, exp. 2.

Biblioteca Nacional (Madrid)

Ca. 1594. *De las costumbras antiguas de los naturales del Piru.* Ms. 3177.

Yale University, Latin American Manuscript Collection (Yale)

1508–1634. *Indice de bullas, brebes, y montorios . . . en el Archivo del Collegio de San Pablo.* Series II, box 2, folder 2.

Archivo General de Indias, Seville (AGI)

1583. Testimony of Diego de Porras Sagreda. Lima, August 30. Audiencia de Lima, legajo 126.

Harkness Collection, Library of Congress (Harkness)

1568. Letter by Antonio López concerning Santiago del Cercado. Peru. Fol. 852r.

Published Works

Acosta, José de. 1954. *De Procuranda Indorum Salute.* 1577. In *Obras de P. José de Acosta,* edited by Francisco de Mateos. Madrid: BAE.
————. 1987. *Historia natural y moral de las indias.* 1590. Edited by José Alcina Franch. Madrid: Historia 16.
————. 2002. *Natural and Moral History of the Indies.* 1590. Edited by Jane E. Mangan. Translated by Frances Lopez-Morillas. Durham: Duke University Press.
Adorno, Rolena. 1998. "Criterios de comprobación: El manuscrito Miccinelli de Nápoles y las crónicas de la conquista del Perú." *Anthropológica* 16:374.
Albó, Xavier. 1998. "La Nueva corónica y buen gobierno: Obra de Guaman Poma o de Jesuitas?" *Anthropológica* 16:307–48.
Alvarado, Juan de. 1965. "Memoria de cosas primeras que acontecieron en los Chachapoyas." 1550. In *Relaciones geográficas,* vol. 4, edited by Marcos Jiménez de la Espada. Madrid: Ediciones Atlas.
Anello Oliva, Giovanni. 1998. *Historia del Reino y Provincias del Perú.* 1631. Edited by Carlos M. Gálvez Peña. Lima: PUCP.
Aronson, Martin. 2002. *Jesus and Lao Tzu: The Parallel Sayings.* New York: Ulysses Press.
Arriaga, Pablo Joseph de. 1968. *The Extirpation of Idolatry in Peru.* Translated and edited by Clark Keating. Lexington: University of Kentucky Press.
Barriga, Victor M. 1954. *Los mercedarios en el Perú en el siglo XVI.* Arequipa: Editorial La Colmena.
Bartra, Enrique. 1967. "Los autores de catecismo del Tercer Concilio Limense." *Mercurio Peruano* 470:359–70.
Bauer, Brian. 1998. *The Sacred Landscape of the Inca.* Austin: University of Texas Press.
Bauer, Brian, and Charles Stanish. 2001. *Ritual and Pilgrimage in the Ancient Andes.* Austin: University of Texas Press.
Bermudez Plata, Cristóbal, ed. 1944. *Catálogo de pasajeros a Indias.* Vol. 3. Seville: CSIC.
Bertoluzza, A., C. Fagnano, M. Rossi, and A. Tinti. 2001. "Primi risultati dell' indagine spettroscopica micro-Raman sui documenti Miccinelli (*Historia et Rudimenta* e *Exsul Immeritus*)." In *Guaman Poma y Blas Valera: Tradición andina e historia colonial,* edited by Francesca Cantú, 181–90. Rome: Antonio Pellicani.

Besom, Thomas. 2009. *Of Summits and Sacrifice: An Ethnohistoric Study of Inka Religious Practices*. Austin: University of Texas Press.

Betanzos, Juan de. 1996. *Narrative of the Incas*. Translated by Roland Hamilton. Austin: University of Texas Press.

Brokaw, Galen. 2003. "The Poetics of Khipu Historiography: Felipe Guaman Poma de Ayala's *Nueva Corónica* and the *Relación de los quipocamayos*." *Latin American Research Review* 38:111–47.

———. 2010. *A History of the Khipu*. Cambridge: Cambridge University Press.

Cabredo, P. R. 1986. "Anua de 1602." In *Monumenta peruana 1966–86*, vol. 8.

Cantú, Francesca, ed. 2001. *Guaman Poma y Blas Valera: Tradición andina e historia colonial*. Rome: Antonio Pellicani.

———. 2002. "Collezionisti e manoscritti andini: Note sui nuovi documenti relativi a Blas Valera." In *Il sacro e el paesaggio nell' American indigena*, edited by Davide Domenici, Carolina Orsini, and Sofia Venturoli, 319–32. Bologna: CLUEB.

Casado Arboniés, Manuel, Antonio Castillo Gómez, Paulina Numhauser, and Emilio Sola, eds. 2006. *Escrituras silenciadas en la época de Cervantes*. Alcalá de Henares: Universidad de Alcalá.

Cieza de León, Pedro. 1985. *El señorío de los incas*. 1553. Madrid: Historia 16.

Cobo, Bernabe. 1983. *History of the Inca Empire*. 1653. Translated by Roland Hamilton. Austin: University of Texas Press, 1983.

———. 1990. *Inca Religion and Customs*. 1653. Translated by Roland Hamilton. Austin: University of Texas Press.

Colajanni, Anonino. 2006. "Los 'defensores de indios' en el Perú del siglo XVI: Escrituras marginadas en favor de la población indígena." In Casado Arboniés et al. 2006, 429–53.

Courson, Barbara Frances Mary Neave. 1879. *The Jesuits: Their Foundation and History*. Vol. 1. New York: Benziger Brothers.

Cronin, Vincent. 1955. *The Wise Man from the West*. New York: Dutton.

———. 1959. *A Pearl to India: The Life of Roberto de Nobili*. New York: Dutton, 1959.

D'Altroy, Terence N. 2002. *The Incas*. Oxford: Blackwell.

Damascene, Hieromonk. 2004. *Christ the Eternal Tao*. Platina, Calif.: St. Herman of Alaska Brotherhood.

Domingo de Santo Tomás. 1560. *Grammática, o arte de la lengua general de los Indios de los Reynos del Perú*. Valladolid.

Durand, José. 1961. "Blas Valera y el Jesuita Anónima." *Estudios Americanos* 109/110:73–74.

———. "Los últimos días de Blas Valera." 1987. In *Libro de homenaje a Aurelio Quesada Sosa*, 409–20. Lima: Villanueva.

Durston, Alan. 2007. *Pastoral Quechua: The History of Christian Translation in Colonial Peru, 1550–1650*. Notre Dame: Notre Dame University Press.

Duviols, Pierre. 1978. "'Camaquen, upani': Un concept animiste des anciens Peruviens." In *Amerikanistische Studien*, edited by Roswith

Hartmann and Udo Oberem, vol. 1, 132–44. St. Augustin: Haus Völker und Kulturen.

Estenssoro, Juan. 1997. "¿Historia de un fraude o fraude histórico?" *Revista de Indias* 57(210): 566–78.

Esteve Barba, Francisco. 1966. "Estudio preliminario." In *Crónicas peruanas de interés indígena*. Madrid: BAE.

Falcón, Francisco. 1918. "Representación . . . sobre los daños y molestias que se hacen a los Indios." 1567. In Urteaga 1918, 135–76.

Fernández García, Enrique. 1990. "Blas Valera es el 'Jesuita Anónimo', autor de la *Relación de las costumbres antiguas de los naturales del Perú*." In *La evangelización del Perú, siglos XVI y XVII*, 217–32. Arequipa: Arzobispado de Arequipa, 1990.

Garcete, Lucio. 2003. "Testimony of Father Lucio Garcete, S.J., to the Inquisitors of Panama City, August 11, 1591 (AHN 1591)." App. B in Hyland 2003, 243–44.

Garcilaso de la Vega. 1987. *Royal Commentaries of the Incas and General History of Peru*. Translated by Harold Livermore. Austin: University of Texas Press.

Gasparotto, Giorgio. 2001. "Studio al microscopio elettronico a scansione (SEM) e microanalisi EDS delle parole chiave metalliche allegate a Exsul Immeritus." In Cantú 2001, 191–94.

Gnerre, Maurizio. 2001. "La telaraña de verdades: El f. 139 del tomo Cast. 33 del Archivum Romanum Societatis Iesu." In Cantú 2001, 195–246.

González de la Rosa, Manuel. 1907. "El Padre Valera, primer historiador Peruano." *Revista Histórica* 2:180–99.

———. 1908. "Los 'Comentarios reales' son la replica de Valera a Sarmiento de Gamboa." *Revista Histórica* 3:296–306.

———. 1909. "Polémica histórica: Las obras del Padre Blas Valera y de Garcilaso." *Revista Histórica* 4:301–11.

Gonzalez Holguín, Diego. 1952. *Vocabulario de la lengua general de todo el Perú llamada lengua Qquichua*. 1608. Lima: Instituto de Historia.

Griffiths, Nicolas. 1996. *The Cross and the Serpent: Religious Repression and Resurgence in Colonial Peru*. Norman: University of Oklahoma Press.

Guaman Poma de Ayala, Felipe. 2009. *The First New Chronicle and Good Government*. 1615. Translated by Roland Hamilton. Austin: University of Texas Press.

Hanh, Thích Nhat. 1995. *Living Buddha, Living Christ*. New York: Riverhead Books.

Hernández, Melchior. 1996. "Memorial de Chiriquí." 1620. In *Religiosos mercedarios en Panamá (1519–1992)*, edited by Juan Zaporta Pallarés, 233–39 Madrid: Revista Estudios.

Horswell, Michael. 2006. *Decolonizing the Sodomite: Queer Tropes of Sexuality in Colonial Andean Culture*. Austin: University of Texas Press.

Hyland, Sabine. 1998. "Illegitimacy and Racial Hierarchy in the Peruvian Priesthood: A Seventeenth-Century Dispute." *Catholic Historical Review* 84 (3): 431–54.

———. 2003. *The Jesuit and the Incas.* Ann Arbor: University of Michigan Press.

———. 2005. "Valera, Falcón y los Mestizos del Perú: Nuevo Testimonio sobre los derechos de los nativos." In *El Silencio Protagonista: El primer siglo Jesuita en el virreinato del Perú, 1567–1667,* edited by Laura Laurencich Minelli and Paulina Numhauser, 127–37. Quito: Abya-Yala.

———. 2007. *The Quito Manuscript: An Inca History Preserved by Fernando de Montesinos.* New Haven: Yale University Press.

Jiménez de la Espada, Marcos, ed. 1879. "Relación de las costumbres antiguas de los naturales del Perú." In *Tres relaciones de antigüedades peruanas,* 136–227. Madrid: M. Tello.

Julien, Catherine. 2000. *Reading Inca History.* Iowa City: University of Iowa Press.

Laurencich Minelli, Laura, ed. 2005. *Exsul Immeritus Blas Valera Populo Suo e Historia et Rudimenta Linguae Piruanorum: Indios, gesuiti e spagnoli en due documenti segreti sul Peru del XVII secolo.* Bologna: CLUEB.

Loaysa, Francisco. 1945. Introduction to Blas Valera, *Las costumbres antiguas del Perú,* edited by Francisco Loaysa. Lima: Domingo Miranda.

Lohmann Villena, Guillermo. 1970. "El licenciado Francisco Falcón (1521–1587)." *Anuario de Estudios Americanos* 27:131–94.

Lopétegui, León. 1942. *El Padre José de Acosta, S.I., y las misiones.* Madrid: Consejo Superior de Investigaciones Científicas, Instituto Gonzalo Fernández de Oviedo.

López, Luis. 1889. "El Visorey Francisco de Toledo." In *Colección de documentos inéditos para la historia de España,* vol. 94, edited by José Sancho Rayon and Francisco de Zadalburu, 472–525.

Loza, Carmen. 1998. "Du bon usage des quipus face a l'administration coloniale espagnole (1500–1600)." *Population* 1–2:139–60.

MacCormack, Sabine. 1991. *Religion in the Andes: Vision and Imagination in Early Colonial Peru.* Princeton: Princeton University Press.

———. 2007. *On the Wings of Time: Rome, the Incas, Spain and Peru.* Princeton: Princeton University Press.

Means, Philip. 1928. *Biblioteca Andina.* New Haven: Yale University Press.

Medina, Borja. 1999. "Blas Valera y la dialéctica 'exclusión-integración' del otro." *Archivum Historicum Societatis Iesu* 68 (136): 229–68.

Métraux, Alfred. 1962. *Les Incas.* Paris: Éditions de Seuil.

Miccinelli, Clara. 1982. *Il Principe de Sansevero: Verità e riabilitazione.* Naples: Società Editrice Napoletana.

Mignolo, Walter. 2002. Commentary on Acosta 2002, 451–518.

Mills, Kenneth. 1997. *Idolatry and Its Enemies: Colonial Andean Religion and Extirpation, 1640–1750.* Princeton: Princeton University Press.

Minamiki, George. 1985. *The Chinese Rites Controversy: From Its Beginning to Modern Times.* Chicago: Loyola University Press.

Miró Quesada, Aurelio. 1971. *El Inca Garcilaso y otros estudios garcilasistas.* Madrid: Cultura Hispánica.

Molina, Tirso de (Gabriel Téllez). 1973–74. *Historia general de la Orden de la Nuestra Señora de las Mercedes.* Edited by Manuel Penedo Rey. 2 vols. Madrid: Provincia de la Merced of Castile.

Montesinos, Fernando. 1882. *Memorias antiguas historiales y políticas del Perú.* Edited by Jiménez de la Espada. Madrid: Miguel Ginesta.

Monumenta Peruana. 1966–86. 8 vols. Edited by Antonio Egaña (vols. 1–6), Antonio Egaña and Enrique Fernández (vol. 7), Enrique Fernández (vol. 8). Rome: MHSI.

Muldoon, James. 1994. *The Americas in the Spanish World Order: The Justification for Conquest in the Seventeenth Century.* Philadelphia: University of Pennsylvania Press.

Mumford, Jeremy. 2000. "Clara Miccinelli's Cabinet of Wonders." *Lingua Franca* 10 (1): 36–45.

———. 2008. "The Inca Legend In Colonial Peru, 1466–1802." *Colonial Latin American Review* 17 (1): 125–41.

Murúa, Martín de. 1987. *Historia general del Perú.* 1590. Edited by Manuel Ballesteros. Madrid: Historia 16.

Nardi, G. 1952. *Conosciamoli meglio: Reduci italiani delle due guerre: 1) Maggiore Riccardo Cera.* Naples: Arti Grafiche dott. Amadio.

Peters, Renata. N.d. "The Anatomical Machines of the Prince of Sansevero." http://www.ucl.ac.uk/~tcrnmrf/machines.htm.

Piras, Guiseppe. 2006. "Martín de Funes (1560–1611): Jesuita rebelde y silenciado." In Casado Arboniés et al. 2006, 273–82.

Porres, Diego de. 1954. "Instrucciones que escribió el P. Fr. Diego de Porres para los sacerdotes que se ocuparon en la doctrina y conversion de los Indios." 1572–1579. In Barriga 1954, vol. 4

Presta, Ana María, and Catherine Julien. 2008. "Polo Ondegardo (ca. 1520–1575)." In *Guide to Documentary Sources for Andean Studies, 1530–1900,* vol. 3, edited by Joanne Pillsbury, 529–35. Norman: University of Oklahoma Press.

Puente Brunke, José de la. 1992. *Encomienda y encomenderos en el Perú.* Seville.

Reinhard, Johan. 2006. *The Ice Maiden: Inca Mummies, Mountain Gods, and Sacred Sites in the Andes.* Washington, D.C.: National Geographic Society.

Relación de idolatrías en Huamachuco por los primeros agustinos. 1918. In Urteaga 1918, 3–56.

Restall, Matthew. 2007. *Seven Myths of the Spanish Conquest.* Oxford: Oxford University Press, 2007.

Ricardo, Antonio. 1951. *Vocabulario y phrasis en la lengua general de los Indios del Perú, llamada Quichua.* 1586. Lima: Instituto de Historia de la Facultad de Letras.

Rocher, Ludo. 1984. *Ezourvedam: A French Veda of the Eighteenth Century.* Philadelphia: John Benjamins.

Salomon, Frank. 1991. "Introductory Essay." In Salomon and Urioste 1991, 1–38.

———. 2004. *The Cord Keepers: Khipus and Cultural Life in a Peruvian Village.* Durham: Duke University Press.

Salomon, Frank, and George Urioste, eds. and trans. 1991. *The Huarochiri Manuscript.* Austin: University of Texas Press.

Sandoval, Alonso. 1647. *Tomo Primero de Instauranda Aethiopum Salute.* Madrid: A. De Paredes.

Sarmiento de Gamboa, Pedro. 2007. *The History of the Incas.* 1572. Translated and edited by Brian Bauer and Vania Smith. Austin: University of Texas Press.

Sharon, Douglas. 1978. *Wizard of the Four Winds: A Shaman's Story.* NY: Free Press.

Solórzano Pereyra, Juan. 1995. *Política Indiana.* Vol. 1. Edited by Francisco Tomás y Valiente and Ana María Barrero. Madrid: Fundación José Antonio de Castro.

Tierney, Brian. 1997. *The Idea of Natural Rights: Studies on Natural Rights, Natural Law, and Church Law, 1150–1625.* Atlanta: Scholars Press.

Urbano, Henrique. 1992. Introduction to Urbano and Sánchez 1992.

Urbano, Henrique, and Ana Sánchez, eds. 1992. *Antigüedades del Perú.* Madrid: Historia 16.

Urteaga, Horacio, ed. 1918. *Informaciones acerca la religion y gobierno de los Incas.* Lima: San Martín.

Urton, Gary. 1981. *At the Crossroads of the Earth and Sky.* Austin: University of Texas Press.

———. 1990. *The History of a Myth: Pacariqtambo and the Origin of the Inkas.* Austin: University of Texas Press.

———. 1999. *Inca Myths.* London: British Museum.

———. 2003. *Signs of the Inka Khipu: Binary Coding in the Andean Knotted String Records.* Austin: University of Texas Press.

Vargas Ugarte, Rubén. 1963. *Historia de la Compañía de Jesús en el Perú.* Vol. 1. Burgos: Aldecoa.

Zoppi, Ugo. 2001. "I documenti Miccinelli: Il contributo offerto dalle analisi radiometriche." In Cantú 2001, 171–80.

Account of the Ancient Customs of the Natives of Peru, An (Valera), 49–103
on *acllas*, 2–3, 79–87
vs. Acosta's views, 6, 36–37
on animal sacrifice, 4 n. 1, 52, 55–56, 59–60, 69, 72, 73–74
authorship of, 5, 105–9
on burial practices, 12, 58–61, 67
on Christianization, 26–27, 88–103
on confession: in Andean religion, 10–11, 66–67, 69–73; in Catholic Church, 96–99, 101
on creation story, 49–51
distortions in, reasons for, 3–4
on God, Quechua word for, 31 n. 6, 49 n. 1
on gods, Andean, 49–52
on *huacas*, 9–10, 52, 56–61
on human sacrifice, 3, 36, 53–56, 106–7
manuscript of: date of, 4–5; discovery of, x, 4; handwritings on, 4, 6, 47; marginalia on, 4, 47; photocopy of, 47
on ministers: diviners, 68–73; *humus* and *nacacs*, 73–74; primary, 63–68
missionaries criticized in, 5
on monks and hermits, 76–79
publication of (1879), 6
on religious orders, 5, 5 n. 3, 94–103
religious universals in, 12–14, 32
on rituals, 10–12
sources used in, 35–44
on superstitions, 87–88
translation of: approach to, 47; text of, 49–103
unique perspective of, 2–4, 14
on Viracocha, 9–10, 49–51
acllahuasi, 8
Aclla mamacona, 84
Aclla mamanchic, 84

acllas (consecrated virgins), 79–87
at Coricancha, 8, 80–81
definition of, 111
duties of, 8, 82, 84–87
menstrual cycles of, 82 n. 51
novitiate of, 80–84, 86, 87
origins of, 80
post-harvest feast held by, 2–3, 85–86, 87
sacrifice of, 36–37, 86–87
after Spanish conquest, 84–85
treatment of, 80, 87
value of virginity of, 90–91
Acosta, José de
censorship of, 20
on challenges of missionary work, 5
on *guadoi*, 111
on hierarchy of civilizations, 37, 43
Historia natural y moral de las Indias, 6, 36–37
on Inca writing system, 43, 43 n. 4
Polo de Ondegardo's influence on, 36–37
on Spanish *vs.* indigenous languages, 31
on transfer of Valera to Europe, 25–26
on transfer of Valera to Potosí, 21
Valera's disagreements with, 6, 36–37
Acquaviva, Claudio
successor to, 29
Valera's punishment decided by, 24, 25, 29–30
Advertencias (Inca), 39
afterlife, in Andean religion, 11–12, 61
Almagro, Diego de, 17
altars, stone, 57, 112
Alvarado, Alonso de, 17–18
Alvarez, Diego, *De titulis regni piruani*, 39, 53 n. 23

amaro, 111
Amaro Toco, 42, 62
Amarucancha, 58, 58 n. 32
amautas, 19, 61, 66, 69, 111
ancestors. *See also* dead, the
  in Andean religion, 11–12
  in Christianity, 12
Andean (Inca) religion, 1–14
  afterlife in, 11–12, 61
  creation stories in, 7, 9, 49–51
  current status of, 7
  the dead in, 11–12, 61–63
  distortions in Valera's presentation of,
    3–4
  diversity of Spanish opinion of, 14
  gods of (*See* gods)
  huacas in, 9–10, 56–61
  local *vs.* state, 6–7
  monks and hermits in, 76–79
  as precursor to Christianity, 3
  priests of (*See* ministers)
  rituals of, 10–12 (*See also specific
    rituals*)
  sacrifice in (*See* animal sacrifice;
    human sacrifice)
  similarities with Christianity, 5, 10
  before Spanish conquest, 6–12
  superstitions in, 87–88
  Valera's respect for, 2, 3
  Valera's study of, 2, 21, 22
Anello Oliva, Giovanni
  censorship of, 20
  on indigenous languages, 31
  "Lives of Men Famous for Their Sanc-
    tity in the Society of Jesus in Peru,"
    27
  on Valera's Quechua vocabulary, 27,
    105, 106
  on Valera's work in Huarochiri, 20–21
Angeles, Mateo de los, *De ritibus indorum*, 39, 53 n. 23
animals
  constellations associated with, 9, 51
  prognostications based on entrails of,
    73–74, 74 n. 42
animal sacrifice
  on behalf of humans, 4 n. 1, 55–56,
    59–60, 87
  in burial practices, 59–60
  in confession, 72

diviners' role in, 69
humus and nacacs in, 73–74
meat from, 74
Polo de Ondegardo on, 36, 37
types of animals in, 52
Annales (Oliva), 39
Anotaciones (Hernández), 38, 53 n. 23,
  72 n. 41
Anotaciones de la lengua (Montoya),
  38–39
anta (tapir), 52, 111
Anta Ayllu (Chanka ruler), 75, 75 n. 44
Anta Huaylla. *See* Anta Ayllu
apachita, 111
apocuna, 111
Apologia pro Indis (Falcón), 38, 53
  nn. 22–23
Appo panaca, 87
Aquaviva, Claudio, 6 n. 5
Arabs. *See* Moors
Aragonés, Falconio, 106
  De libertate indorum servanda, 39
arpai, 112
Asian religions, 12
aspai (aspay), 111
Atahuallpa (Inca emperor)
  baptism of, 107
  brothers of, 53 n. 23, 62 n. 36, 105
  capture and execution of, 17, 27, 62
    n. 36, 90, 90 n. 53
  in civil war, 62 n. 36
  Valera's bias in favor of, 18, 107
  Valera's family connection to, 18
  on worship of humans, 62
aucayoc, 111
Augustine of Hippo, Saint, 37 n. 1
Augustinians, missionary work of, 19,
  95, 101
aurora, 50
Aymara language
  in translation of the *Account*, 47
  Valera's teaching of, 25
  Valera's translation of catechism into,
    22, 25, 31
Aztecs, 37

baptism. *See also* Christianization
  of Atahuallpa, 107
  through force, 88–91
  missionaries performing, 96

Bartholomew, Saint, 57
baths, ritual, 111
Bauer, Brian, 4 n. 1
Bellarmine, Robert, 13
Biblioteca Nacional (Madrid), 4, 47
birds, sacrifice of, 52
Brahminism, 12–13
bread, in harvest feast, 85–86
burial practices
    in Andean religion, 11–12, 58–61, 67
    Spanish destruction of tombs and, 11,
        60, 61

Cádiz (Spain), Valera in, 26
Cajamarca, khipus of, 41
cancha, 111
Cañete, marquis of, 54 n. 25
capac, 111
Capac Hunu, 81
Capac Raymi Amauta (Peruvian king),
    106
Capac Yapanqui Amauta (Peruvian king),
    106
castration, 77–78
catechism, translations of, 22, 25, 31
Catholic Church
    acceptance of indigenous customs in,
        12–14, 32
    conversion to (See Christianization)
    sacraments of, performed by mission-
        aries, 96–99
    shortage of priests in, 92–93, 96
    translations of catechism of, 22, 25, 31
Catuilla, 111
celibacy
    of diviners, 68
    of monks and hermits, 77
    of Vilahoma, 66
    of villca, 68
censorship, of Jesuit writings, 20
Cera, Riccardo, 27
Chachapoyan language, 18
Chachapoyas (city)
    climate of, 17
    Jesuit missions to, 4–5, 102, 102 n. 57
    location of, 17, 18
    Valera in, 17–19
Chachapoyas (people), 18
Chanka nation, 75, 75 nn. 44–45
chasca, 50, 53, 111

chastity. See celibacy
Chaves, Francisco de, 17, 27, 39, 53 n. 23,
    105–6, 105 n. 1
children, sacrifice of, 4 n. 1, 54, 55, 56
chimpu, 111
chinan, 111
Chincha, khipus of, 41
Chinese civilization, 37
Chinese religion, 12, 13
Choque Casa, Cristóbal, 1–2, 3
Christianity
    acceptance of indigenous customs in,
        12–14, 32
    Andean religion as precursor to, 3
    conversion to (See Christianization)
    religious universals in, 12–14
    similarities with Andean religion, 5, 10
Christianization, 88–103
    of acllas, 84–85
    through force, 88–91
    through free will: with instruction,
        94–103; without instruction, 92–94
    indigenous languages in, 30, 31, 92–95
    by Jesuits, 97–103
    Spanish language in, 30–31, 92–93
    struggles of missionaries and Indians
        with, 2
    testing of converts after, 103
    Valera's writings on, 26–27
chucu, 111
chusña, 111
civilizations, hierarchy of, 37, 43
Clement XVI, Pope, 12
cloth, made by acllas, 2–3, 84, 86
clothing
    of acllas, 82, 83
    of local priests, 65 n. 39
    of monks and hermits, 77
    Spanish style of, 31
    of Vilahoma, 63–66
Cobo, Bernabe, 7, 7 n. 9
coca, 52, 111
cocuy, 111
Collasuyu, khipus of, 41
concubines, 90
Condesuyu, khipus of, 41
confession, Andean, 10–11, 69–73
    animal sacrifice in, 72
    confessors' role in, 66–67, 69–73
    khipus used for, 43

confession, Andean (cont'd)
lavations in, 72–73
penances in, 10, 71–72
of thoughts vs. deeds, 11, 71
types of sin in, 11, 70–71
by Vilahoma, 73
Vilahoma's role in, 66–67
by women, 10, 67, 73, 75
confession, Catholic
by Indians, 96–99, 101
shortage of priests for, 96
Confucianism, 12, 13
constellations, 9, 9 n. 10, 51
conversion. See Christianization
cora, 78 n. 47
corasca, 78, 78 n. 47, 111
cori, 111
Coricancha (Cuzco), 8, 79–81
cori uincha, 83
Council of the Indies, 30–31
coya (queen), 50 n. 4, 111
creation stories, 49–51
huacas in, 9
Viracocha in, 7, 49–51
Cuis Manco (Peruvian king), 106
çupay (demon), 51–52, 52 n. 19, 111
cuy (guinea pig), 52, 72, 111
Cuzco
Coricancha (central temple) in, 8, 79–81
Hernández in, 37
human sacrifice in, 4 n. 1
Jesuits' success in, 99–100
khipus of, 41, 42
restoration under Pachacuti VII, 79
Valera in, 2, 21
Viracocha's temple in, 8, 57

dead, the
Andean beliefs about, 11–12, 61–63
resurrection of, 61
worship of, 12, 61
death penalty, for rape, 91
deities. See gods
De las costumbres antiguas de los naturales del Piru. See Account of the Ancient Customs of the Natives of Peru, An
De libertate indorum servanda (Aragonés), 39

demons, in Andean religion, 1–2, 51–52
De ritibus indorum (Angeles), 39, 53 n. 23
De titulis regni piruani (Alvarez), 39, 53 n. 23
Deva, Machin de, 95
Devereux, Robert, 26
devil, the, 41, 49, 52, 69, 78
diet. See food
diviners (huatuc), 68–73, 112
dogs, 52, 53
Domingo de Santo Tomás, 95, 95 n. 54
Dominicans, 5 n. 3, 19, 95, 101
dress. See clothing
Durand, José, 26, 108

Egaña, Antonio de, 108
Ellis, Francis Whyte, 13 n. 11
encomenderos
Alvarez as, 39
critics of, 25
Polo de Ondegardo as, 35
Valera (Luis) as, 18
Enlightenment, 14
Esteban, Onofre, 6, 6 n. 6
Eucharist, 96, 99
eunuchs, 77–78, 84
Exsul immeritus Blas Valera populo suo, 27, 28, 29

Faber, Böhl de, 4
Falcón, Francisco
Alvarez's friendship with, 39
Apologia pro Indis, 38, 53 nn. 22–23
feasts
post-harvest, 2–3, 85–86, 87
for sun god (Inti), 8, 10
Fernández García, Enrique, 5
fire, sacred, 82, 84
firewood, 52
floggings, 24
food
of Incas, 53
of monks and hermits, 77
at post-harvest feast, 85–86
force, Christianization through, 88–91
forgeries, Naples documents as, 28 n. 4
fornication, 23, 25
Franciscans, 19, 29, 95, 101
Fuentes, Miguel de, 23
Funes, Martín de, 25

Garcete, Lucio, 23, 24
Garcia de Castro, Lope, 53 n. 22
Garcilaso de la Vega, 18, 26, 27, 106–8,
  109
glossary, of Quechua terms, 111–13
Gnerre, Maurizio, 29
God, translations of term, 31, 31 n. 6,
  49 n. 1
gods, Andean, 6–10, 49–52. *See also*
  specific gods
  in creation stories, 7–8, 49–51
  as demonic, 1–2
  vs. humans, worship of, 62–63
  local/regional, 6–7
  multitude of, 6–7
  pantheon of, 7–10, 49–51
  state, 7
gold, 18, 76–77, 79
González de la Rosa, Manuel, 8
Gonzalez Holguín, Diego, 111
grammar, politics of, 25, 30
Greece, ancient, 37
Gregory XV, Pope, 13
guacamayas, 111
guadoi, 73, 111
Guaman Poma de Ayala, 28, 29 n. 5
Guanaco, Jesuit missions to, 102, 102
  n. 57
Guayna Capac (Inca emperor), 41
guinea pig *(cuy)*, 52, 72, 111

hahua pacha, 112
hallucinogens, 78 n. 47
hamurpa, 69, 112
Harkness Library, 108
harpay, 112
harvest feast, *acllas* in, 2–3, 85–86, 87
hatun, 112
Hatun Villcas, 69, 70, 74, 76, 81–82, 87
haucha, 112
hauque. See huaoque
hayhuay, 112
heresy
  definitions of, 29–30
  inculturation as, 13
  Jesuits charged with, 19–20, 24–25
  Valera charged with, 20, 24–25, 29
hermits, Indian, 76–79
Hernández, Melchior, 37–38
  Anotaciones, 38, 53 n. 23, 72 n. 41

  career of, 37
  *La interpretación de las oraciones
    antiguas*, 38
  on lavation, 72 n. 41
  as source for the *Account*, 35, 37–38,
    53 n. 22
  writings of, 37–38
Hernández Girón, Francisco, 36, 54 n. 25
hierarchy of civilizations, 37, 43
Hinduism, 12–13, 13 n. 11
"Historia et Rudimenta Linguae Piruanorum," 27
Historia natural y moral de las Indias
  (Acosta), 6, 36–37
Historia occidentalis (Valera), 6, 26
holy places. *See huacas*
Homer, 52
homosexuality, 79 n. 49
huacas (idols or shrines), 9–10, 56–61
  in burial practices, 58–61
  in creation stories, 9
  definition of, 9, 112
  human sacrifice at, 4 n. 1
  importance of concept, 9
  local *vs.* regional, 9
  origins and development of, 56–58
  vs. villcas, 52
huacaylla, 112
huahuas, 56, 87, 112
Huallpa Inga, Juan, 41
huamac, 77, 80, 82, 83, 112
Huamachuco, *khipus* of, 41
huamincas, 51, 112
huampar, 112
Huampar Chucu, 65, 67
huanaco, 112
huancaquilli (hermit), 76–79, 112
huaoque (brother), 62, 112
huapil, 65, 112
huarmi, 112
Huarochiri region
  Lloclluy Huancupa in, 1, 7
  Valera as missionary in, 2, 20–21, 109
Huascar (Inca emperor), 18, 58 n. 32, 62
  n. 36, 107
huaspai. See aspai
huatuc. See diviners
Huayna Capac (Inca emperor), 55 n. 27,
  56, 56 n. 29, 60
huipil. See huapil

human rights, 14
humans, ban on worship of, 62–63
human sacrifice
  the *Account* on lack of, 3, 36, 53–56,
    106–7
  of *acllas*, 36–37, 86–87
  animal sacrifice as substitute for, 4 n. 1,
    55–56, 59–60, 87
  evidence of, 3, 3 n. 1
  in Naples documents, 105 n. 1
  Polo de Ondegardo on, 36–37, 53–54,
    55, 87, 106–7
humus (sorcerers), 73–74, 112
huñicuy, 78, 112
Hunu, 81
hunu, 112

ichuris (confessors), 66–67, 69–73, 112
idols. *See also huacas*
  destruction of, 94–95
  origins of, 51–52
  in temples, 57
Ignatius Loyola, Saint, 19
illa, 31, 31 n. 6, 49 n. 1, 112
illai tanta, 86
Illapa. *See* thunder god
Illa Tecce, 7, 49, 49 n. 1. *See also*
  Viracocha
Inca, Luis, 35, 53 n. 22
  Advertencias, 39
Inca Empire
  Acosta on, 36–37
  Chanka in war with, 75, 75 nn. 44–45
  civil war in, 62 n. 36
  diet in, 53
  gold and silver in, 76–77
  in hierarchy of civilizations, 37, 43
  human sacrifice in, 3, 3 n. 1, 36–37,
    53–56, 106–7
  vs. Moors, 36, 37, 52–53, 73, 111
  religion in (*See* Andean religion;
    Christianization)
  rulers of (*See also specific emperors*):
    chronology of, 50 n. 10, 106; death
    of, 8, 17
  state deities of, 7
  Valera's bias in favor of, 18
  Valera's family connection to, 18
  Valera's study of, 19
  writing system of (*See khipus*)

Inca Yupanqui (Inca ruler), 75, 75 n. 45
inculturation, 12–14, 32
India, inculturation in, 12–13, 13 n. 11
Indians. *See also* Inca Empire
  encomenderos' mistreatment of, 25
  missionaries' mistreatment of, 5
  Valera's bias in favor of Incas *vs.* other,
    18
indigenous languages. *See also specific*
    languages
  in instruction of converts, 30, 31, 92–95
  politics of, 29–32
  Spanish language as replacement for,
    30–31
  translations of catechism into, 22, 25, 31
indigenous peoples. *See* Indians
indigenous religions. *See also* Andean
    religion
  Christianity's acceptance of customs of,
    12–14
  similarities with Christianity, 12
Inquisition. *See* Spanish Inquisition
inspections, by *Vilahoma*, 66
interpretación de las oraciones antiguas,
    La (Hernández), 38
Inti. *See* sun god
intip, 112
Inti Raymi (feast), 8, 10
Itinerario (Jofre), 39, 53 nn. 22–23

Jesuit Provincial Catalogues, 17, 18, 108
Jesuits, 97–103
  arrival in Peru (1568), 19, 97
  in authorship of Naples documents, 29
  in authorship of the *Account*, 5, 108–9
  censorship of writings of, 20
  Chachapoyas missions of, 4–5, 102, 102
    n. 57
  establishment of order, 19
  inculturation attempted by, 12–14, 32
  on *khipus*, 43
  mestizo members of, 20, 22
  methods of, 99–101
  opposition to work of, 97–102
  in Spanish Inquisition, 19–20, 23–24
  success of Christianization by, 97–103
  vs. Theatines, 19 n. 1
  threats to survival of, 19
  transfers among parishes, 22
  Valera's life as, 19–29

Jiménez de la Espada, Marcos, 6, 108
Jofre, Marcos, 106
  Itinerario, 39, 53 nn. 22–23
Juli
  Montoya in, 39
  Valera in, 21, 26, 39
Jupiter (god), 50, 51 n. 15

khipukamayus, 40, 41, 42
khipus
  on *acllas*, 82–83, 84, 86
  alternative spellings of, 40
  authors of, 41
  definition of, 27, 40, 113
  functions of, 40–44
  location of, 41
  in missionary work, 43, 43 n. 3
  among Naples documents, 27, 28
  as source for the *Account*, 35, 40–44
  after Spanish conquest, 42–43

Latin language
  in translation of the *Account*, 47
  Valera's knowledge of, 20, 21, 30
lavations, 72–73
Lima
  Falcón in, 38
  Spanish Inquisition in, 23 n. 2
  Valera's move to, 22
  Valera under house arrest in, 6, 22–26
Lima, Councils of, 91
Lima Council of Bishops, 36, 38, 39, 43 n. 3
Lima Episcopal Council, 42
"Lives of Men Famous for Their Sanctity
  in the Society of Jesus in Peru"
  (Anello Oliva), 27
llamas, 9, 55, 56, 59–60, 112
Lloclluy Huancupa (god), 1–2, 7
Loaisa, Hierónimo de, 97
Loaysa, Francisco, 5
Lohmann Villena, Guillermo, 40
Lopétegui, León, 5
López, Cristóbal, 95
López, Luis, 23–24, 108–9
Loza, Carmen Beatriz, 42
Luke (biblical book), 100 n. 55

MacCormack, Sabine, 36
Madrid (Spain), Biblioteca Nacional in,
  4, 47

Malagá (Spain), Valera in, 26, 27
mama aclla, 84
mamaconas, 80, 81, 83, 84, 112
mamanchic, 84
Mama Quilla. *See* moon god
Manco Capac, 106
map, of western South America, xi
marriage
  of *acllas*, 81, 83, 84, 86, 87
  equal rank in, 86
  missionaries performing, 96
  after Spanish conquest, 91
Mars (god), 51, 51 n. 15
Mass, 96
Means, Philip, 5
Medina, Borja de, 29
Méndez, Cristóbal, 26
menstrual cycles, 82 n. 51
Mercedarians, 19, 43 n. 3, 101
Mercury (god), 51, 51 n. 15
mestizos
  Hernández as, 37, 38
  in Jesuit order, 20, 22
  Valera as, 2, 18, 20–21, 38, 108
Métraux, Alfred, 5
Miccinelli, Clara, 27, 28 n. 4, 105 n. 1
Miccinelli documents. *See* Naples
  documents
ministers (priests), Andean, 63–76
  acllas as, 80
  in burial practices, 11
  clothing of, 65 n. 39
  at Coricancha, 79–80
  demotion of, 63, 75–76
  diviners as, 68–73
  humus and *nacacs* as, 73–74
  lineage of, 8, 66, 75
  obedience of, 76
  primary, 63–68 (*See also* Vilahoma)
  selection process for, 74–75
  types of, 63, 67–68
  women as, 75
missionary work
  the *Account*'s criticism of, 5
  in Chachapoyas, 4–5, 102, 102 n. 57
  Christianization through, 94–103
  as demotion, 95–96, 101
  in Huarochiri region, 2, 20–21, 109
  inculturation in, 12–14, 32
  indigenous languages in, 94–95

confession, Andean (cont'd)
  khipus in, 43, 43 n. 3
  orders involved in, 19, 95
  Molina, Cristóbal de, 39, 95   .
mollo shells, 52, 112
monks. See also religious orders
  Indian, 76–79
  Vilahoma compared to, 3, 63, 66
Montalvo, Gregorio de, 95
Montalvo, Juan de, 39
Montesinos, Fernando de, 50 nn. 9–10,
  106
Montoya, Juan de, Anotaciones de la
  lengua, 38–39
moon, in creation stories, 49–50
moon god (Mama Quilla), 8, 79
Moors, vs. Incas
  Polo de Ondegardo on, 36, 37, 52–53,
    73
  ritual baths of, 111
Morillo, Hernando, 6, 6 n. 5
Mumford, Jeremy, 28 n. 4
mummification, 11–12, 58, 61
music, in animal sacrifice, 74

nacacs (butchers), 73–74, 112
Naples (Miccinelli) documents, 27–29, 28
  n. 4, 105 n. 1
Nardi, G., 27
native peoples. See Indians
natural rights, 14
New Chronicle and Good Government
  (Guaman Poma), 28, 29 n. 5
nina, 112
Nina Villca, 82, 84
Nina Villca, Sebastian de Quispe, 2, 109
Nobili, Roberto de, 12–14, 13 n. 11
Nombre de Jesús, 21, 41
ñusta, 112

obedience
  of ministers, 76
  of monks and hermits, 78
Oliva, Juan de, 53 nn. 22–23, 106
  Annales, 39
Olivares, Diego de, 39, 53 n. 23, 105, 106
opacuna, 72, 73, 111, 112
oracles, 69
orcos, 112
osno (altar), 57, 112

pacaric, 112
Pacari Tampu, khipus of, 41
Pachacamac, khipus of, 41
Pachacuti VII (Inca emperor), 79–80, 79
  n. 49, 106
Pachacuti IX (Inca emperor), 79, 106
paco, 112
pampacuna, 112
Panama Inquisition, 23
Pantaleón, Juan de, 95
pasña, 112
penances, 10, 71–72
Perez, Francisca, 18
Peru. See also Spanish conquest of Peru
  chronology of kings of, 50 n. 10, 106
  Jesuits' arrival in (1568), 19, 97
  origins of name, 49, 107–8
Philip II (king of Spain), 19
Pirua (god)
  the Account on, 49, 50, 50 n. 9, 108
  Hernández on, 38
  Montesinos on, 50 nn. 9–10
  temple of, 58
pirua (granary), 42, 107–8, 112
Pirua Pacaric Capac (Peruvian king), 106
Pirua Pacaric Manco Inca (Peruvian
  king), 50, 50 n. 10, 106
Pizarro, Francisco, 17, 27
Pizarro, Gonzalo, 95
Pizarro, María, 23, 108
Polo de Ondegardo, 35–37
  the Account's criticism of, 35, 36–37
  on acllas, 80, 87
  arrival in Peru, 54 n. 24
  career of, 35–36
  gold and silver sought by, 76–77
  on human sacrifice, 36–37, 53–54, 55,
    87, 106–7
  influence of, 36, 54
  on Moors vs. Incas, 36, 37, 52–53, 73
  on penances for the poor, 71
  on resurrection of the dead, 61
  on worship of humans, 62
  writings of, 36
popes, Vilahoma compared to, 63, 63
  n. 38
Porres, Diego de, 43 n. 3
Potosí
  Hernández in, 37, 38
  Valera in, 21–22, 38

poverty
  of monks and hermits, 78
  and penances, 71–72
prayers, *khipus* used in, 43, 43 n. 3
prelates, 67–68
priests, Andean. *See* ministers; *Vilahoma*
priests, Catholic, shortage of, 92–93, 96
primary ministers, 63–68
prisoners, Inca treatment of, 55
puberty ritual, 81–82, 81 n. 50
pucyu, 113
pumas, 52
punchao, 113
Punchao (Day) statue, 8

Qhapaq ucha ceremony, 3 n. 1
Quechua language
  in Christianization, 30, 31
  glossary of, 111–13
  God in, word for, 31 n. 6, 49 n. 1
  Hernández's writings on, 37, 38, 38
    n. 2
  Montoya's writings on, 39
  politics of using, 30–32
  Polo de Ondegardo's understanding of,
    87
  in translation of the *Account*, 47
  Valera's knowledge of, 18
  Valera's teaching of, 22, 25
  Valera's translation of catechism into,
    22
  Valera's writings on, 27, 30, 105, 106
quichuchicuy, 81–82, 81 n. 50, 113
quipos. See khipus
quipus. See khipus
Quishuarcancha, 8
quispi, 113
Quitaya, Valera in, 18
Quito
  khipus of, 41
  Valera in, 5–6, 26, 27
Quito Manuscript, 106

rape, 23–24, 25, 91
Raqchi, temple of, 8
reciprocity, in rituals, 3, 9
Reinhard, Joahan, 3 n. 1
religion(s). *See also* Andean religion;
  Christianity
  universals in, 12–14

religious conversion. *See* Christianization
religious orders. *See also* monks; *specific
  orders*
  the *Account* on, 5, 5 n. 3, 94–103
  differences of opinion on heresy, 29–30
  resurrection of the dead, 61
Ricardo, Antonio, 111
Ricci, Matteo, 12–14
rituals, 10–12. *See also specific types*
  hallucinogens in, 78 n. 47
  reciprocity in, 3, 9
Rodríguez de Aldana, Catalina, 18, 19
Roman Curia, 24
Rome, ancient, 37
Royal Commentaries of the Incas (Garcilaso de la Vega), 26
runa, 55, 56, 113
runap camac, 9

Saboya, Amadeo de, 27
sacraments, performed by missionaries,
  96–99
sacrifice. *See* animal sacrifice; human
  sacrifice
Sacsahuaman, *khipus* of, 41, 42
salt, 18
Sánchez, Ana, 47
Sanmartino, Giuseppe, 28 n. 4
Sansevero, Raimondi de Sangro, prince
  of, 28 n. 4
Sanskrit language, 13
Santiago del Cercado
  church of Saint Blas in, 98
  establishment of, 97–98, 108
  Valera in, 21, 108, 109
Saturn (god), 51, 51 n. 15
Savoya-Aosta family, 27
sayri (tobacco), 52, 113
sepulchers. *See* tombs
servants, of Viracocha, 51
shamans, hallucinogens used by, 78 n. 47
sheep, 52
shrines. *See also* huacas
  khipus kept at, 41
silver, 76–77
sin. *See also* confession; vices
  in thought *vs.* deed, 11, 71
  types of, 11, 70–71
snakes, 52
Society of Jesus. *See* Jesuits

sodomy, 79 n. 49
Solórzano Pereyra, Juan, 31, 32
South America, map of western, xi
Spain
    Jesuits in, 19
    Valera in, 6, 6 n. 5, 25–27
Spanish conquest of Peru
    acllas after, 84–85
    Andean religion before, 6–12
    destruction of tombs in, 11, 60, 61
    diversity of opinion in, 14
    gold and silver in, 76–77
    khipus after, 42–43
    spiritual conquest in, 2 (*See also*
      Christianization)
    Valera's criticism of, 27
    Valera's family in, 17–18
    value of virginity after, 90–91
    vices of Spaniards in, 89–91, 94
Spanish Crown
    Jesuits threatened by, 19–20
    on Spanish language, 30–31
Spanish Inquisition
    diversity of opinion in Peru on, 14
    Jesuit house in Lima used by, 23 n. 2
    Jesuits in, 19–20, 23–24
    rape as crime in, 23–24, 108
    Valera as prisoner of, 23
Spanish language
    in instruction of converts, 30–31,
      92–93
    politics of, 30–32
    as replacement for indigenous lan-
      guages, 30–31
    in translations of catechism, 22
suicide, 59
sun, in creation stories, 49–50
sun god (Inti), 7, 8
    acllas in worship of, 8, 80
    origins of worship of, 79
    temple of, 8, 57, 79
supay, 41, 52 n. 19
superstitions, 87–88

tampu, 113
tanta, 113
tapir, 52
Tarma, *khipus* of, 41
tecce, 113
temples, 56–63. *See also huacas*

construction of, 57
Coricancha, 8, 79–81
    of moon god, 8
    natural, 56–57
    of Pirua, 58
    of sun god, 8, 57
    of thunder god, 9
    of Viracocha, 8, 57
Theatines, 19 n. 1
thunder god (Illapa), 8–9
Ticci Viracocha, 7, 7 n. 9
Titicaca, Lake, 7, 8
Tito Atauchi, 53 n. 23, 105
titoy, 78, 113
Tito Yupanqui. *See* Inca Yupanqui
tobacco, 52, 113
tocapu, 113
tocrico, 113
tomariy, 113
tombs
    in Andean religion, 58–61
    Spanish destruction of, 11, 60, 61
Tommasi, Emilio di, 27
Topa Inca Yupanqui (Inca emperor), 55,
    55 n. 27, 63, 75
translations
    of catechism into indigenous lan-
      guages, 22, 25, 31
    politics of, 29–32
*Tratado y averiguación sobre los errores
    y supersticiones de los Indios* (Polo
    de Ondegardo), 36
Trujillo, Valera in, 18–19
Tupac Amaru (Inca emperor), 37

universals, religious, 12–14
Urbano, Henrique, 5, 47
urcu, 113
Urton, Gary, 40–41, 82 n. 51
uscacuy, 78, 113
uscavillullu, 77
Uscovilca. *See* Anta Ayllu
utirayay, 69
utopian communities, 25

Valera, Blas, 17–32. *See also Account of
    the Ancient Customs of the Natives
    of Peru*
    as author of the *Account*, 5, 105–9
    birth of, 17, 18

career as Jesuit, 19–29
  on Christianization, 2, 26–27
  death of, x, 26, 27, 28, 108
  distortions in presentation of Andean
    religion, 3–4
  early life of, 17–19
  education of, 18–19
  heresy charges against, 20, 24–25, 29
  Historia occidentalis, 6, 26
  under house arrest in Lima, 6, 22–26
  in Huarochiri mission, 2, 20–21, 109
  on human sacrifice, 106–7
  illness of, 6, 24, 25–26
  language classes taught by, 22, 25
  as mestizo, 2, 18, 20–21, 38, 108
  in Naples (Miccinelli) documents,
    27–29
  parents of, 2, 17–19, 20–21
  politics of translations and, 29–32
  respect for Andean religion, 2, 3
  in Spain, 6, 6 n. 5, 25–27
  study of Andean religion, 2, 21, 22
  transfers among parishes, 21–22
  translations of catechism by, 22, 25, 31
  writings of, 26–29, 105–9; lost works,
    26, 105; suppression of, 13
Valera, Jerónimo, 18
Valera, Luis, 17–19, 39, 53 n. 23, 105
Valladolid, Spanish Inquisition in, 19–20,
    24
Vargas Ugarte, Rubén, 23
Varro, Marcus Terentius, 37 n. 1, 109
Veda, "fifth," 13 n. 11
Vedantic Hinduism, 13
Veiled Christ, The (Sanmartino), 28 n. 4
vices
  of Indian converts, 93–94, 96
  of Spaniards, 89–91, 94
vicuña wool, 86
vila, 113
Vilahoma (high priest), 63–68
  clothing of, 63–66
  compared to monk, 3, 63, 66
  compared to pope, 63, 63 n. 38
  confession by, 73
  confessors selected by, 66–67

death of, 67
definition of, 113
demotion of, 63, 75–76
election of, 63, 67
functions of, 63, 66–67
income of, 63, 66, 75–76
inspections by, 66
lineage of, 8, 66
in novitiate of acllas, 81–82, 83, 87
in sun worship, 8
use of term, 63 n. 38
villcas, 31, 52, 68, 113
villulluy, 78, 113
violence, Christianization through, 88–91
Viracocha (god), 7–8
  the Account on, 9–10, 49–51
  in creation stories, 7–8, 49–51
  definition of, 113
  Hernández on, 38
  names of, 7, 7 n. 9, 49
  servants of, 51
  temple of, 8, 57
Viracocha Inga (Inca emperor), 75, 75
    n. 43
Virgil, 52
virginity, value of, 90–91
virgins, consecrated. See acllas
Vitelleschi, Muzio, 29
Voltaire, 13 n. 11

wilderness, penance in, 10, 71–72
women
  confession by, 10, 67, 73, 75
  as consecrated virgins (See acllas)
  as ministers, 75
  value of virginity of, 90–91
wool, 86
writing system, Inca. See khipus

Yacana constellation, 9
yana villcas, 68, 74, 76, 82, 113
Yutu Inga, Francisco, 41
yuyac, 56, 113

Zárate, Agustín de, 35
Zuidema, R. T., 29

latin american originals

Series Editor | Matthew Restall

This series features primary source texts on colonial and nineteenth-century Latin America, translated into English, in slim, accessible, affordable editions that also make scholarly contributions. Most of these sources are being published in English for the first time, and represent an alternative to the traditional texts on early Latin America. The initial focus is on the conquest period in sixteenth-century Spanish America, but subsequent volumes include Brazil, as well as later centuries. The series features archival documents and printed sources originally in Spanish, Portuguese, Latin, and various Native American languages. The contributing authors are historians, anthropologists, art historians, and scholars of literature.

Matthew Restall is Edwin Erle Sparks Professor of Latin American History and Anthropology, and Director of Latin American Studies, at the Pennsylvania State University. He is co-editor of *Ethnohistory* journal. J. Michael Francis is Professor of Latin American History at the University of North Florida.

Associate Series Editor | J. Michael Francis

Board of Editorial Consultants
Noble David Cook | Edward F. Fischer | Susan Kellogg
Elizabeth W. Kiddy | Kris E. Lane | Alida C. Metcalf
Susan Schroeder | John F. Schwaller | Ben Vinson III

Titles in print
Invading Colombia: Spanish Accounts of the
Gonzalo Jiménez de Quesada Expedition of Conquest (LAO 1)
J. Michael Francis

Invading Guatemala: Spanish, Nahua,
and Maya Accounts of the Conquest Wars (LAO 2)
Matthew Restall and Florine G. L. Asselbergs

The Conquest on Trial: Carvajal's "Complaint
of the Indians in the Court of Death" (LAO 3)
Carlos A. Jáuregui

Defending the Conquest: Bernardo
de Vargas Machuca's "Apologetic Discourses" (LAO 4)
Edited by Kris Lane and Translated by Timothy F. Johnson

Forgotten Franciscans: Writings from an Inquisitional Theorist,
a Heretic, and an Inquisitional Deputy (LAO 5)
Martin Austin Nesvig

Gods of the Andes: An Early Jesuit Account
of Inca Religion and Andean Christianity (LAO 6)
Sabine Hyland